PENART

THE GARDEN BY T

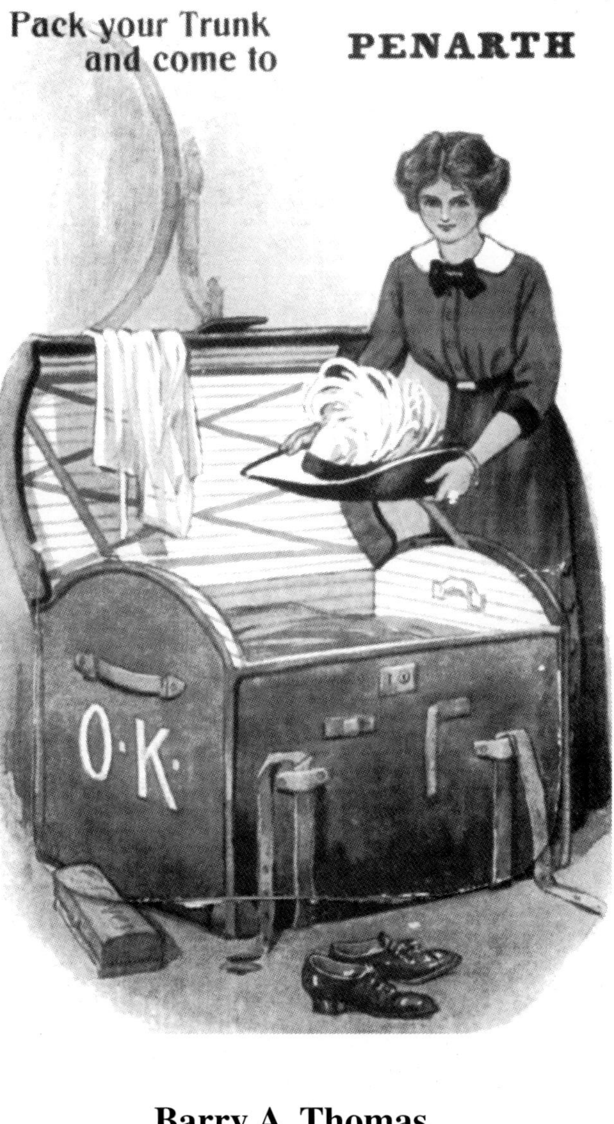

Barry A. Thomas

Alexandra Park looking towards the Esplanade Hotel and the sea.

PENARTH

THE GARDEN BY THE SEA

BY

Barry A. Thomas

Published by Barry A. Thomas
1997

Published in Great Britain by Barry A. Thomas, 1997

ISBN 0 9532197 0 4

Ynys Einion
Eglwys Fach
Machynlleth
SY20 8SX

Printed by J & P Davison, James Place, Treforest, Pontypridd.

for
Lynda, Marc & Len

ACKNOWLEDGEMENTS

I would like to thank the Editor of the Penarth Times for permission to reproduce many of the illustrations that I have included. Also the Vale of Glamorgan, the Glamorgan County Records and Camlin, Lonsdale (Landscape Architects, Llangadfan, Powys) for allowing me to include copies of their documents amd plans.

CONTENTS

ACKNOWLEDGEMENTS vi

INTRODUCTION viii

THE BEGINNINGS OF PENARTH 1

VICTORIAN AND EDWARDIAN DEVELOPMENTS
AT THE SEA FRONT 16

THE SECOND PHASE OF DEVELOPMENT 1911-1939 46

THE SECOND WORLD WAR YEARS 1939-1945 94

THE POST WAR PERIOD 98

TOWN PARKS AND OPEN SPACES 122

BIBLIOGRAPHY 143

INTRODUCTION

Ornamental and pleasure gardens have been prepared and tended in Britain since the arrival of the Romans. Parks and gardens were created in increasing numbers from the Middle Ages, but they were all associated with castles and rich land owners until the industrial revolution of the last century. The movement of large numbers of country people into urban communities led to the need for open spaces, or public parks, within the expanding and overcrowded towns and cities. The first urban parks were essentially open recreational areas for the local people and it was much later that parks were developed to attract visitors. Beaches, of course, have always been popular places to visit for those people fortunate enough to live near the coast

The first urban park in Wales to be opened to the public was Cardiff's Sophia Gardens in 1855. Others soon followed in the rapidly expanding boom-time South Wales towns. Penarth was one of these new towns that grew throughout the latter part of the last century and the early part of this one. Coal, railways and shipping created wealth and the *nouveaux riches* wanted somewhere grand and pleasant to live. Robert Forrest, the agent for the Windsor Family, exploited this need and developed the town to his plan. Penarth soon had the best concentration of Victorian buildings in South Wales and was a town that could only be truly rivalled by distant Tenby. Its new esplanade was beautifully framed by high ground and lovely parks that gave little room for visual intrusions. Then came the obligatory pier with the chance for people to walk over the sea or take an excursion on a paddle steamer. All this was done without funfair or side-show attractions and only quality entertainment was allowed in the parks and on the pier. Penarth soon became known as *The most beautiful little town in South Wales.* It was a sea side town with class. My grandmother who went to live in Barry, from Whitland via Porth, thought Penarth to be ever so posh. Robert Forrest would have approved.

This book sets out to write the history of the sea side development and of the parks and to set them in the context of the townís own development. Even though the planning ravages of the 1960s and 1990s have destroyed many lovely old buildings we are fortunate that most of the town has survived intact to the present day.

THE BEGINNINGS OF PENARTH

About one hundred and fifty years ago Penarth was only a cluster of whitewashed cottages and farmhouses with a population of only 105. An inventory on a land schedule annexe for Penarth Manor in 1752 listed 18 tenants and three cottages worth a total of £228. Cardiff was seven miles away by way of Leckwith Moors and Llandough, although quicker access could, if necessary, be had via the rope-ferry over the River Ely or by the rowing boats and sailing boats that plied between Cardiff and Penarth beach.

At that time the beach was largely undeveloped. There was no promenade and the only access was down the old Beach Road, by the paths through the wooded dingles, or by boat from Cardiff Pier Head. Nevertheless the beach was still a great attraction and on Sundays and other fine days there was a constant stream of people making their way back and fore along it, picnicking, and swimming in the sea. The south-east facing beach then, as now, was protected from most of the prevailing winds by the cliff and gave spectacular views all the way from the Steep and Flat Holms, Brean Down and Weston-super-Mare to Clevedon. Seaside development was limited to Balcony Villa, Sea Cot, the Lifeboat Station with their small stretches of sea wall and a piece of embankment in front of Sea Cot. A Mr Withers, who lived in a nearby cottage did, however, let out bathing machines and supplied teas. Above the cliff were Plymouth House (now Bron-y-Glyn) built in 1861 and the coastguard station and cottages built in 1864. One of the local sights was of the coastguards walking along the shingle with their long telescopes slung over their shoulders. They were a natural target for small boys who wanted to look through their telescopes.

This outwardly idyllic rural scene was soon to change. The mines in the South Wales valleys were seeking more efficient ways of exporting their much valued coal because the docks were not large enough to cope. In 1853 an idea was put forward by John Batchelor to enclose the whole of the bay from Penarth Head to Cardiff Docks that included diverting the Taff across the moors to the Ely and the construction of a tunnel below Cogan Pill to take off surplus water to Sully. It would be controlled by a harbour trust financed by the Bute Trustees, the Taff Vale Railway and the merchant community. This forerunner of the Cardiff Bay Barrage scheme was thought to be far too Utopian to succeed and was quickly dropped.

Congestion in the Cardiff Bute Docks and the favoured treatment of the Rhymney Railway eventually led the Taff Vale Railway to seek an independent outlet to the sea. A partnership was sought with the Hon. Windsor Clive who owned the land alongside the mouth of the river Ely. This land and, indeed, the Manor of Penarth, St Fagans Castle and much other land in Glamorgan had come to the family on the marriage of the Earl of Plymouth to Elizabeth Lewis. In return, a payment of £40,000 was made to her father, Thomas Lewis, for all his

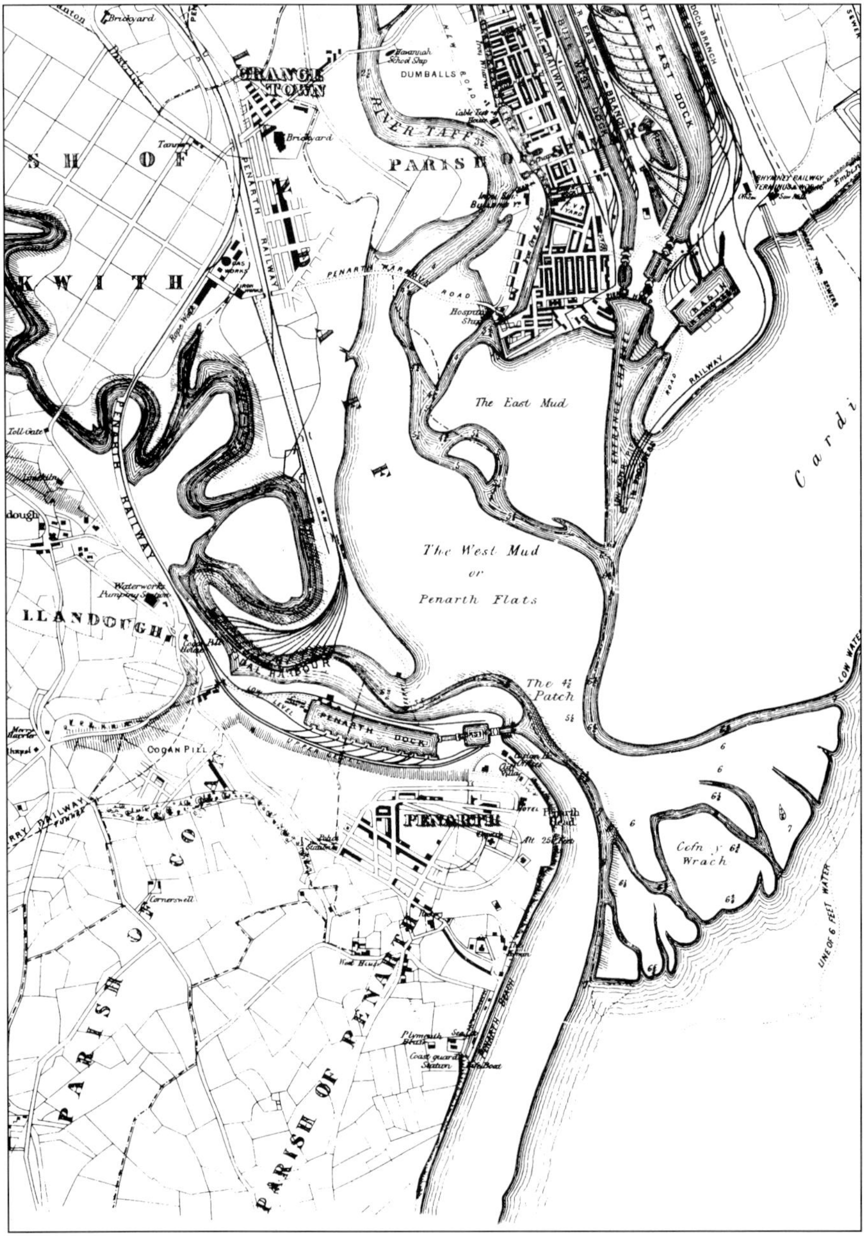

Penarth in 1869 by T.Waring. The Penarth Railway runs on the east side of the River Ely to the Tidal Harbour and crosses the river higher up to run to Penarth Dock. Penarth itself is largely confined to the headland side of Windsor Road (County Archives).

Glamorgan Estates, and an arrangement giving him the right to make use of them during his life. Thomas Lewis had himself obtained power of attorney to receive possession of the Manor of Penarth from the Dean and Chapter of the Holy Undivided Trinity Cathedral Church in Bristol in 1711.

In 1856 the Ely Tidal Harbour and Railway Act (21st June 1856) then authorised the construction of a railway and tidal harbour on the eastern bank (Cardiff side) of the river Ely. In 1859, 10 tidal coal berths and an iron ore discharging stage were opened at a cost of £137,000. There was the intention to bring passenger trains from Cardiff to end on the Cardiff side of the harbour where there would be a large hotel. A small Penarth Railway Hotel was built, but it is now known as the Red House.

This plan was soon realised to be too small to meet the growing demand for coal exports, so the Penarth Harbour Dock and Railway Company was formed and received permission, through the Penarth Harbour Dock and Railway Act (27th July 1857) to construct a dock at the mouth of the Ely at Penarth. The Act also authorised the construction of a branch railway to link up to the Taff Vale Railway at Grangetown. The directors of all three companies were mainly the same people, including Crawshay Bailey, Thomas Powell, John Nixon, James Insole and John Batchelor, with Windsor Clive supplying the land and £100,000 and Samuel Dobson as the architect. The Dock opened in 1865 and Penarth was never the same again. A grand Custom House, since described as pompous baroquely classical, was built in 1865 to match the aspirations of the Dock owners. It was built of rusticated stone and cream coloured brick with Corinthian pilasters, pedimented gables, a dome and a massive clock. Next to it was built a three storey terrace in bold French renaissance style. Penarth Dock quickly became a successful and busy port leading to its necessary extension in 1881 for the steady increase in shipping. One million cubic yards of soil and rock were removed as the Dock was extended into a hillside. The total expenditure for the Dock was approximately £1,250,000. The town and its population grew with the Docks. There were 1,406 people noted in the 1861 census and the population then doubled every ten years until the end of the century. In 1908 a floating pontoon was constructed in the dock for general ship repairs.

The first buildings had centred around the north side of Windsor Road with houses in Glebe Street, Salop Street, Ludlow Street and a few in John Street and Maughn Terrace. At this time the only way to Cardiff was by ferry across the Ely or by the horse-drawn bus service that started in 1865. This slow growth was soon to change with the coming of the railway. The dock's branch railway was extended into the town as the Cardiff, Penarth and Barry Junction Railway, with Penarth Town Station opened on February 27th 1878 by the Honourable Clive Windsor M.P. The station was surrounded by fields with a farm house standing on the site of the present day Turner House Gallery. The nearest block of buildings was at the coast guard station. At this time the railway was a single

An aerial view across Cog Moors in 1971 showing the proposed new river channel and the sites for the refuse tips. The fan-like railway to the old Tidal Harbour is still visible in the foreground as are some wharfs (Penarth Times).

Penarth Docks at the turn of the century (Penarth Times).

track as far as Llandough and Penarth Station itself only consisted of the Cardiff arrival platform (the Plymouth Road side). The trains had five small coaches and ran about eight times a day. Later, it was extended to Sully and linked to the Barry Railway at Biglis junction, Cadoxton. The railway was nominally independent but it was always managed and run by the Taff Vale Railway.

The new town station opened up what was to become the south-eastern part of the town for development. Within twenty years it was laid out with broad tree-lined roads for the larger houses of wealthy ship owners and well-to-do businessmen who could now commute to Cardiff easily by train. Impressive houses built from many local materials soon spread along the top of the cliff and around the wooded dingles that led down to the beach. Some are of dark Pennant Sandstone from the coal field, others of light grey Liassic limestone from local quarries such as Cwrt-y-Vil, red brick from Cogan Marl or yellow brick from small quarries within the town and nearly all were finished with Bath Stone finishing. Although the Windsors controlled much of the early development there seemed to have been no overall detailed plan for the town which ended up with a loose network of streets rather than a geometric pattern. There only appears to be more planned development in the vicinity of St Augustine's Church.

Looking northwards along Marine Parade. This high class housing was almost certainly built to the design of the Windsor Estate architect, Mr H. Snell.

"Might the weary merchant raise
His mansion where to end his days
And here regain that long-lost health
Spent 'mid the toils of heaping wealth."

from the *Bristol Mercury* Guide to Penarth (1884)

The increasing number of ships and the larger tonnage they carried led inexorably to innumerable transient sailors dependent on local boarding houses. The sailors were usually paid off at the end of the journey often with large amounts of money and wanting liquor and women. Many public houses and commercial hotels were built to cater for the needs of the sailors and the men who worked in the dock which led to numerous instances of drunkenness and riotous behaviour in the early days of the town. Fear of drunken lawlessness showed itself quite clearly in August 1881 when the building next to the Railway Station (now the Station Hotel) was refused a licence. This was because the Local Board did not want 'frequent scenes of riot and disorder, especially during the tourist season, close to the high class villas and houses' and people 'causing obstruction to the station entrance'.

The Marine Hotel which stood under Penarth Head at the seaward end of the Dock Building.

Several more exclusive hotels were built for the more discerning businessmen and sea captains. The earliest was the Penarth Hotel built by the Taff Vale Railway in 1868 at a cost of £27,000. However, even though it was set in 20 acres, with a bowling green, lawn tennis courts and archery butts, it was not a commercial success because it was too far from the town centre and the beach. It was bought by Mrs Gladys Gibbs (née Morel) as a memorial to her husband who was killed in action in 1917 and reopened as a branch of the National Children's Home. In 1936 it became the Headlands School. The Lansdowne Hotel built opposite the town station in 1886 was much more viable although the most commercially successful hotel of all was the Esplanade Hotel built on the Esplanade in 1887.

The Penarth Hotel.

LOVETT'S

WINDSOR HOTEL AND STEAM BREWERY

PENARTH, NEAR CARDIFF

ESTABLISHED 1856 - THE ONLY BREWERY IN THE TOWN

Visitors to this Fashionable Resort will do well to try this celebrated

HOME-BREWED BEER

Made solely from Pure Spring Water, Malt and Hops – In casks 1½, 9, 18, 35 & 54 gal.

Talk not of Fiz or Sherry, for this at least is clear
There's not a beverage in the land Like Lovett's Home Brewed Beer.
It braces you, it wakens you, it fills you with good cheer.
It's meat, and drink, and clothes, I think is Lovett's Home Brewed Beer.
Whene'er you put it to your lips such Hoppy flavours rise,
In fancy the green lanes of Kent spring up before your eyes.
It's flavoury, it's savoury, as amber it is clear
As far's I think, there's not a drink like Lovett's Shilling Beer.

A draught of Stout is good no doubt, and so's a glass of wine.
And "Mountain Dew" is something too, a favourite of mine.
But good as all these potions are, as daylight it is clear
Nought can surpass a foaming glass of Lovett's Home Brewed Beer.
Then take your Claret and your Hock, if these things suit your taste.
Or quaff a Bumper of Champagne, if that you think is best:
It's a free country, take your choice, mine's evident and clear see,
There it sprkles, here's your health, in Lovett's Home Brewed Beer.

Agent for S. Allsopp & Son's Burton-on-Trent Ales and Stout
Prices and Terms on application

Families supplied with the Finest Brands of Wines and Spirits at Wholesale Prices. Sample order will oblige. Choice Cigars.

Please note the address:

Windsor Hotel and Brewery, Maughan St. and Windsor Rd., Penarth, near Cardiff

An advertisment for the Windsor Hotel and Steam Brewery in the 1884 Bristol Mercury Guide to Penarth.

The town centre itself expanded, with Glebe Street becoming completely inadequate as a shopping street. A new shopping centre was planned for Arcot street but this never occurred. Instead, the residential houses at the upper end of Windsor Road were converted into shops by building projecting fronts into the gardens. Windsor Arcade and the adjoining Lloyds Bank were built in 1898. The major blot on the Windsor Road landscape was then only a piece of enclosed land in front of the St Fagans Hotel. In 1900 the owner agreed to give it to the Council on the understanding that the cost would be borne by the town. This transfer enabled the Winsdor Road redevelopment to be completed. Penarth became one of the most fashionable towns in South Wales.

Being fashionable and successful brought the town one further problem. Penarth needed its own cemetery. The Council approached Lord Windsor who agreed to sell 5 acres for this purpose at £450 an acre. The Council agreed and the cemetery was laid out.

The junction of Windsor Road and Bradshaw Place about 1910.

By the turn of the century there were more than ten millionaires living in Penarth in their large exclusive houses. Shipping magnets, such as John Cory, Sven Hanson, Thomas Morel and John Batchelor, all lived where they could see the Bristol Channel and their own ships approaching and leaving Cardiff and Penarth Docks. Mr Pyke-Thomson, who had made his fortune from flour, built Redlands in Plymouth Road and then, in 1888, opened the Turner House Gallery on the corner of his land at the entrance to the dingle leading down to the beach. The Gallery is now part of the National Museums and Galleries of Wales.

The Turner Gallery was designed by Edwin Sewards (of Seward & Thomas, Cardiff) as virtually one room divided horizontally into two levels by a continuous balcony (post-marked 1905).

The Paget rooms were built in 1906 to the rather radical design of John Coates Carter. The frontage shows no sign of the roof and the large room with its balcony is both pleasant and functional. The rooms were named after Lord Windsor's wife whom he married in 1883. John Coates Carter also designed All Saints Church in Victoria Road in 1890, and again in 1927 after fire destroyed it, and the Church Hall in 1906. He also designed a number of houses in that part of Penarth including the Red House in Victoria Road. This was built in 1902 for himself and his Swiss wife, hence the wide steeply sloping roof and the full length balcony.

Religion and education were important to the lives of most Penarth residents. Large churches of several denominations were constructed in Penarth and the work of the churches and chapels stretched out into many other aspects of people's lives. Many of the churches and chapels were designed by eminent architects of the time. St. Augustine's by William Butterfield, All Saints and its Church Hall by John Coates Carter, the Tabernacle in Plassey Street by Jones and Thomley, Christ Church Congregational Chapel by Habershon and Fawckner.

St Augustine's Church on Penarth Headland. This building replaced an older church which had its foundations in the late 12th century. Baroness Windsor met the £10,000 cost and gave the extra land necessary for its construction in 1885-6. The town had to have a church to match the grand scale of the planned town. It was designed by the celebrated church architect William Butterfield in 'functional Gothic'. Its interior of multicloured brickwork in geometric patterns make it the best example of Butterworth's 'polychromic' churches (post-marked 1909).

The Presbyterian Curch in Wales English Conference was held in Penarth (September 20th 1905) at the Prebyterian Church in Plassey Street. It has been replaced by the Jehovah's Witnesses Assembly Hall.

A Church Lads Brigade camp on the Cliff Fields in 1907.

The first publicly controlled school was Albert Road School which opened in 1876. The gothic style of the original building was designed by Henry C. Harris but John Coates Carter was responsible for the later extensions with art nouveau decorated panels on the gable ends.

A sewing class in Albert Road School in 1899 (County Archives).

Penarth's first cinema in Glebe Street in 1910 run by Oliver Willmore and his brother. Admission was 2d, 4d and 6d and when the seating was full extra space was provided behind the screen where the audience saw the films as a mirror image (Penarth Times).

Ready for a charabanc excursion (Penarth Times).

Many private schools were also built, because the more affluent residents preferred to send their children to a school of their choosing. One of these was the Penarth Tutorial College for boys which was built in 1896 in a prime position at the junction of Stanwell Road and Hickman Road. This, however, was not one of the schools destined for long-term survival and in 1922 it was converted into the Washington Hotel, so named to attract the increasing numbers of Americans visiting the town. It was in fact built with American dollars. The owner, Captain Beavan had rescued the American millionaire Mr. Vanderbilt whose yacht was trapped on a reef. The yacht was towed free and Mr. Vanderbilt showed his appreciation with a large cheque, whereupon Captain Beavan gave up the sea to settle in Penarth. Even the hotel was not very successful and in 1932 the Washington cinema (now the Washington Gallery and Low Cost) was built on the tennis courts and the Washington shops on its car park.

The Washington Hotel and the public Library.

The Public Library Act of 1882 was adopted by the Council to establish their Free Library Committee in 1894. That year they agreed to take over the premises of Mr Davies in Arcot Street for a library and reading room. The present library was opened in 1905 on a site donated by Lord Windsor. The Carnegie Trust gave £4,000 for its construction and the architect was Harry Snell. Robert Forrest donated the clock. In 1909 the Council decided that it could now afford to build the planned caretaker's cottage adjoining the library and agreed to spend up to £350 on its construction.

Societies and clubs flourished in the town to cater for the varied interests of the more well-to-do townspeople. There were of course the Yacht Club and the exclusive Tennis Club in Rectory Road (on land given by Lord Windsor), but there were also clubs for specialist interests such as gardening or history. Singing was popular and the Penarth Male Voice Choir was formed in September 1896.

The judges and committee of the Penarth May Show, 1914.

The Penarth History Society (date unknown).

The success of the town was, therefore, brought about by several interrelated factors that combined to leave a legacy of refinement and prosperity. They were not just the development of the docks and the extension of the railway into the town, but rather the result of the vision of the Windsors (later the Earls of Plymouth). It was their wish to make Penarth into a beautiful town to live in, as well as a centre of commerce and trade, that determined so much of the present day layout of the town. Of course it must be remembered that the family was a major stockholder of the Docks and the Taff Vale Railway and owned much of the land upon which the town was being built, so they were able to make a substantial return upon their investments.

Much of the early planning in Penarth was the responsibility of the Estate Agent, Robert Forrest, who was in sole charge of the Glamorgan part of the Windsor estates. In May 1875 the Windsor estate helped establish the Penarth Local Board to include the parishes of Penarth, Cogan and Llandough by transferring to it some of the estate's administrative responsibilities. The Windsors promptly handed over to them all the main drainage and the principal roads from 40ft to 60 ft wide which had been constructed at a cost of about £100,000. Robert Forrest, in his new even more powerful position as the first chairman, set about developing and transforming the embryonic town. Forrest soon realised that it was vital to upgrade the appearance of the beach and the surrounding land if Lord Windsor's plans for the town were to succeed. He was convinced that access and facilities were poor, the refreshment facilities were inadequate, thought that the donkeys for hire were monopolising the top of the beach and believed that bathing and the drying of costumes should be controlled and moved to one end of the beach. In an 1876 letter he talked about the Beach being crowded with a perfect rabble from the hills and other places. He went on to suggest that 'Mr Morgan's tea gardens, the donkeys, donkey boys, stalls for ginger beer, buns etc. and Mr Matthew's refreshment rooms have become a perfect nuisance by obstructing the legitimate use of the Beach and preventing those people whom it ought to be our study to draw to Penarth from enjoying its privileges.' Then added 'we cannot stop the rabble coming to Penarth but we can throw obstacles in the way of their getting accommodation and that may have the desired effect in the end. My aim is to increase the comforts of the residents and legitimate visitors and entice respectable people to come here to reside.' The activities of the day trippers from Cardiff and the valleys had to be curtailed. Forrest's subsequent actions to develop the sea front were to transform the town into a more gentile and refined resort that would attract what he considered to be a better class of resident and visitor.

VICTORIAN AND EDWARDIAN DEVELOPMENTS AT THE SEA FRONT

Windsor Gardens

It was during the early development of Penarth that Lord Windsor and Robert Forrest started work on the first of the parks that were to give the town so much appeal in the years to come. The first, more northerly, section of this planned garden was opened in 1880. This stretch of cliff-top garden, overlooking the Bristol Channel, was entered from the seaward, bottom end of Bridgeman Road, which could be easily reached by horse-drawn cab from the station. The entry fee of one penny was collected by the garden superintendent who lived in the brick-built house that still stands just inside the gardens. Residents of Penarth and visitors could now stroll on good pathways in pleasant surroundings, with sea views and sea breezes, removed from the bathers, donkeys and rowdiness of the beach. I suspect that the superintendent exercised his own discretion in deciding who was permitted to pay the penny for entry. The residents of Bridgeman Road and Marine Parade, whose gardens abutted on the new garden, were permitted to have their own private entry gates on the payment of half a guinea. Some of these private gates are still in place although the present residents have no right to use them. Many of these houses had their own rather splendid gardens that were laid out by Charles Jones, a local landscape gardener who was also responsible for laying out the gardens of Penarth House.

The Bridgeman Road entrance to Windsor Gardens.

The garden was designed by Robert Forrest, and Lord Windsor's architect, Henry Snell, who worked from the Estate Office at no. 3 Windsor Terrace. Lawns and flower beds were laid out and shrubs and trees planted. The 1884 Guide to Penarth published by the *Bristol Mercury* described the garden as: ìThe central broad walk is flanked by groves, shrubberies, flower beds and clusters of bright golden gorse, both the Spanish and English species of which grow here magnificently. But the place is noted for its fresh and luxuriant foliage. The arbutus grows freely - the chestnuts, the ash, the beech and in sheltered places the silver birch flourish well - laurels abound ...... the pyrus japonica blossoms in profusion, and the more tender plants and shrubs - as well as the visitors themselves - are protected by the thick growth of hawthorn fringing the cliffs seaward. Welcome seats are placed in inviting nooks, and in summer the band of the local volunteers plays in the orchestra. The entrance is by ornate and picturesque Elizabethan lodge.' Most noticeable today are the foreign Oaks and the Willow-leaved Pear near the bandstand and the remaining one of the pair of Monterey Cypresses above Cliff Road. Some are probably part of the original plantings.

The Bandstand in Windsor Gardens early this century.

Looking south along Windsor Gardens towards the bandstand and the bridge (post-marked 1910).

At first the garden extended to the dingle where the path led down from the coastguard houses and the newer Marine Parade to the original 1861 lifeboat station at the southern end of the beach. The visitors, if they wished, could leave the garden at the dingle by a one-way gate.

Windsor Gardens were then extended southwards in 1885 to the top of the newly constructed Cliff Hill road via a splendid ornate timber bridge that spanned the dingle - described at the time as 'the verdant slopes of which are bright with gorse and the cream-coloured blossoms of vigorous grown broom.' The gardens then had an overall area of 4.5 acres and a second brick-built lodge was built at the new southern entrance. Some sections of the original protecting iron railings that were put on the cliff-edge of the gardens are still there and can be seen to have been made by D. Evans of Llandaff in 1885. A bandstand was installed to enhance the use of the gardens and concerts were regularly held there during the summer months. Two cannon from the Boer War were later placed in the garden with their barrels pointing out to sea.

Looking northwards along Windsor Gardens over the bridge towards Penarth Head. Plymouth House can be seen on the left (post-marked 1905).

On the bridge in Windsor Gardens (post-marked 1911).

At this time there was plenty of activity on the beach even though it was severely regulated. There was a donkey stand at the very northern end of the beach and bathing machines were at the southern end. But remember, this was 1880 and mixed bathing was frowned on, especially by the Penarth Board. They decreed that gentlemen bathing should be defined by a line from the rocket mast, lying south of the boat houses (where the Italian Gardens are today), and that no gentlemen should be permitted to the north of this line where ladies bathing machines were located. Because of these regulations, many local people preferred to walk along the cliffs to St Mary's Well Bay to swim, or to swim from the Dock beach even though it was becoming steadily polluted by rubbish and coal dust. Byelaws were introduced at the same time for the pleasure boats operating from the beach.

As the Windsor Gardens were being laid out, the Windsor Estate was simultaneously undertaking other developments that would establish the future design of the sea front. Cliff Hill was cut out of the cliff in the early 1880s by the removal of 40,000 cubic yards of rock which were used for the foundations of the new 36 foot-wide esplanade that was built from beneath the Kymin to the boat house; all at a total cost of about £10,000. Now there was a comfortable place to go for a seaside walk without having to stumble over pebbles while avoiding the donkeys, bathers and picnickers. The Windsor estate had 'improved' Penarth's sea front as part of the overall scheme to upmarket the town. Access to the beach was via the ramps at either end of the esplanade or down one of the three flights of wooden steps between the pier and the yacht club. The Penarth Local Board approved the Windsor Esplanade (as it was then called) and Cliff Hill for they quickly accepted them as Highways to be maintained at public expense (but remember that Robert Forrest was both the Estate Agent and the Chairman of the Local Board). Lord Windsor gave further money which enabled the Local Board to purchase 24 seats and 12 park seats for £74.5s.0d. The number of people visiting the new Esplanade continued to increase and soon the number of seats was completely inadequate. So in 1899 the Council purchased some more.

Cliff Hill not only gave access to the beach from the more southerly developments of the town but it opened up a circular route for the horse-drawn cabs. They could now leave the rank opposite the town railway station, go along Rectory Road and down Beach Road to the Esplanade making their return journey up Cliff Hill, along Marine Parade and Plymouth Road to the station. By 1894 there were 19 hackney carriage licenses in Penarth with the drivers having their own shelter in front of the town station. Unfortunately the cabmen did not look after the shelter to the satisfaction of the town council who were complaining about its state and imposed a new set of rules for its use. Licencing and control was certainly the order of the day. In October that year three boatmen had their licences cancelled because they had operated on Sundays. The police were also being urged to stop traders obstructing the Esplanade with their hand trucks and carts.

The horse-drawn cabs were of course for the more well-to-do visitors arriving by train, but the majority of people walked down to the beach. There was originally an unmarked footpath leading to the beach through the attractive wooded valley immediately opposite the station, but the ever increasing numbers of visitors coming to the town by rail prompted the Windsor Estate to construct a proper footpath to control the access. This new path through the Dingle was opened in 1883 giving a much more pleasant walk from Plymouth Road and the station down to Windsor Gardens, the new esplanade and the beach. Two wooden bridges were constructed across the stream, steps were built up to Park Road and gas lamps installed to light the path in 1884. The local board took over this path, the Kymin path and the Cliff path as public highways in June 1886. At first the path that led down a slope from Plymouth Road was gravel, but in 1903 asphalt was laid as an experiment and soon proved to be very popular. The shallow steps, known either as the dolly steps or the hobble steps, were then cut into the top slope a couple of years later

A winter scene in the Dingle after the winter snows in January 1909.

The original wooden upper bridge on the Dingle path. The slope from Plymouth Road is without its present-day steps (post-marked 1904).

The original wooden lower bridge on the Dingle path. The steps to Park Road can be seen in the background (post-marked 1907).

The Dingle bridges were replaced with reinforced concrete ones by Mr George Chapman in 1910 at a cost of £500. Some of the original path-side iron railings and one of the original iron gas lamps (now electric) still remain.

The new concrete upper bridge and the flight of steps.

The new concrete lower bridge. The two boys are in Alexandra Park. The steps on the other side of the bridge lead up to Park Road (dated 4/11/04).

The Yacht Club and Baths

Further developments soon followed for the benefit of the local residents and to tempt more visitors to the town. The Penarth Boat Club, which changed its name to the Penarth Yacht Club in 1885, was established on the site of the lifeboat station. The lifeboat was moved to a new position under Penarth Head, near the Custom House, where it stayed until 1905 when difficulties in launching prompted the R.N.L.I. to move the station to Barry. The impressive Yacht Club building, which still stands, was constructed in three phases in 1884, 1885, and 1905 and its slipway was built at the same time as the Esplanade.

In October 1881, the Local Board adopted the Baths and Wash Houses Acts for the purpose of constructing seawater baths at Penarth. By January 1883 the plans were laid, the Windsor Estate had promised £2,000 and the rest of the capital was secured by a loan. The swimming baths were built on the Esplanade in 1884 and cost £7,500, being constructed to the design of Henry Cornelius Harris, surveyor to Penarth, and Henry Snell who were paid a commission of 2.5% for preparing the plans and supervising the work. The central octagonal tower with its cupola was designed to be both a chimney and a water tower. There were two swimming baths, in which sea water was used as it was thought to be beneficial to health, and hot and cold freshwater slipper baths. In winter the larger bath was boarded over and used as a gymnasium and roller-skating rink. The sea water for the swimming baths was pumped from the beach to open 70,000 gallon concrete tanks in the field (later Alexandra Park) behind the baths. The water then passed into a precipitation tank where a new technique of introducing a small jet of lime water made the clay coagulate so it could be filtered out. The water then flowed by gravity into the baths.

The baths were opened in the summer of 1885. The tariff that was set for entry seems quite high for the time so the intention seems to have been to provide an exclusive venue. They were:

1st class salt water swimming bath				8d
2nd class	"	"	"	3d
1st class salt water slipper bath				1s
2nd class	"	"	"	8d
1st class hot or cold fresh water bath				6d
2nd class	"	"	"	3d

All the sessions were naturally single sex and there was no suggestion that mixed bathing would be provided. A Manager of Baths was hired to ensure smooth functioning and, as was usual in such cases, his wife was also expected to work. Such a system did not, however, always work well. In October 1908, the manager resigned with immediate effect following 'a complaint'. The advertisement that followed clearly stated that the Manager/Instructor should be married and his wife competent to take charge of ladies' swimming and other classes.

A mixture of sailing and steam ships in Penarth Docks at the turn of the century. The wooden jetties of the Ely River Tidal Harbour are on the right.

A Taff Vale train leaving Cogan Station for Cardiff. The docks with the coal-loading derricks are in the background and the Barry line in the foreground.

*The horse-drawn coach from Cardiff proceeding up Windsor Road.
Not all the converted houses have extended shop fronts yet.*

The public library in Stanwell Road. Behind the library is Christchurch Congregational Chapel built in 1897 to the design of Habershon and Fawckener. It was the best example of a Gothic Chapel in Penarth with a spire reaching 110 ft. Nevertheless, it was demolished on Sunday March 12th, 1989 and replaced by the present row of shops and offices (post-marked 1908).

Windsor Gardens at the turn of the century. The view is looking northwards over the iron bridge towards Penarth Headland (post-marked 1907).

On the Windsor Gardens bridge. A New Year card sent in 1906. The pier and a paddle steamer can be seen in the background.

The bridge linking the two parts of the Windsor Gardens. Penarth House stands behind the bridge. The building to the right is the Penarth Yacht Club on the Esplanade where the lifeboat station originally stood. The boat is probably decorated for a regatta. The path leads down from Marine Parade and the old coastguard station (post-marked 1908).

The Yacht Club (post-marked 1908)

A view from the pier towards the shore with the Baths, the Marine Hotel and the old route of Beach Road to the right (post-marked 1911).

A view from the pier with Balcony Villa, Rock Villa and the Esplanade Buildings to the left (post-marked 1908).

A painting by Fred Childs showing The Lady Margaret, in Campbell's livery, cruising off Penarth in 1901. This ship was built in 1895 for a company consisting largely of the Directors of the Pier Company although it was managed by Edwards and Robertson of Cardiff. At the end of the 1895 season, Edwards and Robertson sold their own vessels to to John Gurn of Cardiff and the Lady Margaret was sold to P. & A. Campbell Ltd.

P. & A. Campbell's Bristol Channel Passenger Steamers. The Glen Rosa is entering Ilfracombe harbour. The Ravenswood is probably off Penarth (post-marked 1905).

Alexandra Park soon after it opened. The bandstand, shelter, seats and low limestone walls all stand out in the rather bare open park in this uphill view.

Looking towards the pier from Alexandra Park.

The upper entrance to Alexandra Park soon after it was opened (postmarked 1909).

A view in Alexandra Park showing one of the cannon positioned just above the shelter; another is just out of view on the left. Three of the imposing houses in Bridgeman Road can be seen to the right of the shelter. (post-marked 1907).

On Cliff Walk (post-marked 1920).

Enjoying the view on Cliff Walk. Penarth Head can be seen in the background.

Strolling on Cliff Walk at the turn of the century.

Boats underneath Penarth Head (post-marked 1905).

An amusing postcard (postmarked 1910).

A novelty card with pull-out views of Penarth (post-marked 1913).

The Esplanade and beach viewed northwards from the Pier. This pre-1902 view shows the landing stage for the Cardiff/Penarth ferry in the foreground and refreshment tents further along the beach.

The Esplanade viewed southwards from the Pier showing Cliff Hill Road in the background. Wooden steps lead down to the beach and the waiting pleasure boats. These boats were licensed and regulated by the Town Council and, although popular with the visitors, the owners were not allowed to ply for hire on Sundays.

The Penarth Ferry - the Iona - leaving Cardiff Pier Head for Penarth (post-marked 1906).

The Pier with its pavilion. The horse-drawn cabs are waiting for passengers returning to the station. A paddle steamer is approaching the Pier (post-marked 1916).

The pier and beach from the entrance to Cliff Walk. In the foreground are tents and bathing machines (post-marked 1905).

People on the beach watching a waiting to board the paddle steamer (post-marked 1909).

A turn of the century view of the Pier with a departing Campbell's steamer, the Lady Margaret, crowded with passengers. A Bristol Channel pilot cutter at the end of the pier is preparing to sail (post-marked 1904).

The pier entrance with Penarth Head in the background (post-marked 1904).

In 1886 a few more facilities were provided in the form of a drinking fountain and a horse trough. Some money from Lord Windsor also led to the erection of public urinals and a ladies 'retiring room'.

The Pier

The end of the last century was also the age of pier building and Penarth clearly needed one to add to its seaside attractions. The first attempt to construct a pier in Penarth was in the early 1880s by a London firm who laid the foundations and erected a number of iron columns before running out of money. The Penarth Promenade and Landing Pier Company Limited was then established in 1888 by a consortium of local businessmen, including the shipping magnates John Cory and Thomas Morel and the brewer E. Hancock, with the help of Robert Forrest for Lord Windsor, and a nominal charge of £25 per annum for the foreshore use by the Windsor Estate. Local enthusiasm was high although there was concern over the delay in starting its construction. Work on the pier was eventually restarted in 1894 by the engineer, H. F. Edwards and the Manchester contractor, James and Arthur Mayoh. The Mayoh Brothers were clearly in demand because they were also constructing the Brighton Palace Pier and the Morecambe West Pier. Mumbles was to be the next on their list and then came the Grand Pier at Weston. The structure with its landing stage was completed and officially opened in April 1895. The Company also owned and operated a number of small boats which were kept in their boat house and boat yard opposite the pier at the corner of Bridgeman Road and the Esplanade. They also had exclusive rights over the use of an area of beach on both sides of the pier.

The pier and a paddle steamer photographed from the Baths. A pre-1902 card because the back is solely for the addresss.

The pier quickly added to the attractions of this seaside part of the town even though it was only 658 feet long and, therefore, left high and dry at low tides. It was unfortunate that the pier was not extended another 50 feet to give greater depth for the Channel steamers, but the Pier Order prevented it being longer in case it obstructed the entrance channel to Cardiff and Penarth Docks.

The pier was to serve two purposes: To provide an interesting and supposedly healthy place to walk, for which an entrance fee was set at 2d, and as a landing stage for the paddle steamer pleasure boats which were starting to operate throughout the Bristol Channel in increasing numbers. Since the Bonnie Doon began operating in the Bristol Channel in 1886, eight other paddle steamers had been put into service. All the several rival companies wanted to use Penarth's new pier and the ships often raced each other to the landing stage to pick up the waiting crowds. The Pier had only been open for a couple of weeks before the Council Clerk was directed to write to the companies operating the paddle steamers asking them to approach the pier at slower speed to minimise the risk of accidents with the small boats plying from the beach. Operating the steamers was, however, a reasonably risky venture and gradually the number of companies decreased until P. & A. Campbell eventually became the dominant and then the sole company in the Bristol Channel.

A view of the sea front from the end of the pier. To the left are Balcony Villa and Rock Villa and behind them the imposing houses of Bridgemen Road. To the right are the Swimming Baths. The field behind the baths shows the photograph to be pre-1902. The x on the card was put by the sender to mark where she lived. This is the Windsor Gardens Lodge so her father must have been the Park Keeper (post-marked 1904).

Two views towards the sea front. The upper shows the bandstand and shelter in Alexandra Park above the pier shelter (post-marked 1904). The lower shows the Esplanade Hotel on the right. The sea front block of shops on the left shows the photograph to be post 1904 (postmarked 1913).

The Promenade and the pier were a great success and visitors started to come in ever increasing numbers. In 1897 two important people visited Penarth. One of these was Guglielmo Marconi who, in May that year, sent the first radio transmission over water from Lavernock Point to Flat Holm. Marconi had arrived in England in 1896 and first conducted experiments between the General Post Office in London and the Thames Embankment. He then transfered to Salisbury Plain before coming to Penarth in May 1897. The choice of venue had been determined by the need to undertake comparative experiments with those that Sir William Preece had made in the area. Preece had used the so-called 'parallel wire' method while Marconi used his 'elevated aerial' system. After Marconi transmitted, Preece acknowledged the superiority of the new system. A memorial plaque to Marconi was placed in Lavernock church wall in May 1947 by the Cardiff Rotary Club and a monument was erected at the spot where he transmitted in May 1997. Unfortunately, thieves have recently stolen the plaque and ornate metal tops to the railings surrounding one of the churchyard graves. A great loss.

Barry Amateur Radio Club in period costume, in May 1997, re-enacting Marconi's first transmission from Lavernock (Penarth Times).

The second person was the great French impressionist painter Alfred Sisley who came to Penarth on the 9th of July to paint landscapes from the cliff tops. He stayed in Penarth until the middle of August working on a series of paintings from the cliffs to the south of the town. A number of factors brought Sisley to the town. Although born in France, his parents were British which gave him a British passport. His patron, Francois Depeaux was a Rouen industrialist who had business interests in Cardiff. He had no doubt suggested to Sisley that a visit would be worthwhile.

Sisley also brought with him his mistress, Eugenie Lescoueze, with whom he had been living for over 30 years. As they had been living as a married couple in France for many years, marriage in that country was clearly out of the question, especially as Sisley was trying to become a naturalised Frenchman. They married in Cardiff registry office that summer.

After leaving Penarth, Sisley and his new wife moved on to Langland Bay where he completed two more sets of paintings.

The Cliff at Penarth, the evening, low tide (La falaise à Penarth, le soir, marée by Alfred Sisley 1897; now belonging to the National Museums and Galleries of Wales. Sisley painted this view from the start of the cliff walk looking southwards with the island of Steep Holm on the left. The tide tables reveal that Sisley must have set up his easel between July 22nd and 25th to see this evening view (National Museums and Galleries of Wales).

By 1902 an estimated 25,000 people visited the town with many coming from far away by train and by boat.

Passengers aboard the Devonia - September 6th, 1913.

Children on the beach.

The pier with its pavilion, tea room and departing paddle steamer photographed from the Esplanade Hotel.

An aerial view of the pier with its pavilion at the seaward end and the tea rooms at the landward end.

Refinement naturally still prevailed. The pier was open for promenading and for steamer trips but nothing else was allowed. There were certainly no amusements of any kind allowed on the pier or esplanade. Organised entertainment was another matter and soon daily shows were being held on the roof of the Esplanade Shelter, Cliff Walk, Penarth Head, the north end of the Esplanade under the Kymin and especially on the pier. For ten years these shows were held in the open or under canvas, but in 1907 a wooden pavilion, called the Bijou, was finally built at the far end of the pier. At last there was a permanent place for shows and reviews. Bathing machines were available at the southern end of the beach for the more adventurous visitors.

Fredrick Speed.

The Council decided to increase visitor facilities at the beach by constructing a Public Shelter with proper toilets. Eventually it was opened in 1903, but not before the Council was complaining about inactivity by the contractor who was blaming the late delivery of the ironwork from Glasgow. The Council had thought of building a caretaker's cottage but dropped the idea because of the cost. That year the Council also produced an official 72 page guide book to encourage more visitors. This was *Penarth Illustrated*, which contained road and footpath maps and 68 photographs.

Then a block of shops and flats were built on the sea front by Fredrick Speed of Shepton Mallet who had previously built the Lansdowne Hotel block opposite the station in Plymouth Road and the British Legion building in Station Approach. They were first discussed by the Council in 1901 and completed in 1904 on land that had been sold to the Council in 1902 and at a rent of 5/- per foot per annum. In order to clear the land for building Speed had to dynamite the cliffs. When completed this new Esplanade block included private hotels at each end: Govier's restaurant at the northern end and the Gwalia Cafe at the southern end.

The Esplanade looking towards the new (but not yet completed) block of hotels, shops and flats (post-marked 1904).

Balcony Villa photographed from the pier at high tide. To the right of the Villa is the shed and boat yard belonging to the Pier Company. Behind the Villa is the Windsor Garden Lodge and two houses in Bridgeman Road.

A view of the Esplanade after the construction of the public shelter (left) and the block of shops in 1904.

Visitors to Penarth certainly had a variety of places in which to eat. Apart from the new block of shops on the esplanade, there was the Esplanade Hotel, Salter's Cafe and Tea Gardens on the pier and the refreshment stalls on the beach to the north of the pier. Near the station, the Washington Hotel offered luncheon at 4/- and dinner at 5/- which must have been aimed at the better-off visitor. It was also advertising luxurious accommodation with hot and cold water in every bedroom, an electric lift to all floors and up-to-date central heating in all rooms at a price of $4\frac{1}{2}$ guineas for full board and 7 guineas for two persons. They also had accommodation for cars in the Hotel grounds. There was also the more modest Glendale next to the path leading down to the beach. Nevertheless, many people continued to picnic on the beach much to the annoyance of the shopkeepers who objected to what they saw as hordes of the less desirable sort of people spending little or nothing in their shops and restaurants. Interestingly, the refreshment tents did not last very long because in 1908 the Earl of Plymouth refused permission for their erection on the foreshore.

Govier's restaurant and the Beach Cliff private hotel (post-marked 1906).

In 1907 the Earl offered to sell the piece of land adjacent to the Shelter, but the Council declined the offer. The next year the Earl did agree to the construction of a children's paddling pool to be constructed on the beach for the nominal rent of 5/- *per annum*. The Council borrowed £220 for the purpose, but before work was started, Mr Collett offered in July 1921 to construct the pool free of charge. The Council accepted, but it was a couple more years before work was started.

The Council naturally maintained a strict protocol with the Windsor family at all times. In October 1905 an illuminated address was presented to the Honourable Windsor Clive on the occassion of his coming of age and in November that year a letter was sent congratulating him on his Earldom. Then, on Friday April 1st 1910, the Penarth Council, the Cricket Club and the tenants of the Windsor Estate went to St Fagans Castle to present an address of congratulations to Lord Windsor on having his majority. He was now Ivor Miles Windsor-Clive - Lord Windsor. The Council arrived at St Fagans at about 3-30, the Town Clerk read the address and the Chairman, Mr T. H. Mondy JP presented it to Lord Windsor. Within, it contained 'The interests of your family have been so intimately associated with the general well-being and prosperity of Penarth, that the Council, on behalf of the inhabitants of the District, desire to express the hope that these interests may long continue.'

Visitor numbers were increasing all the time and the Council was constantly discussing ways of improving the facilities without destroying the very essence of refinement. In October 1910 their attention turned to the Esplanade itself because it was so congested, especially on holidays, that it was thought to be dangerous. Enlargement of the Esplanade over the foreshore seemed to be the best option. The idea was to construct a promenade on pillars made from beach stones covered with cement. It was also thought desirable for the Council to own the foreshore. It was the estimated price of £6,000 that prevented them pursuing the idea and then the War years intervened. It was many more years before this embryonic idea was turned into reality.

A Beach Inspector was hired at a wage of 28/- a week and it was his job to ensure that everyone obeyed the byelaws and created no nuisance. This appointment was mirrored in the town where there was an Inspector of Nuisance, who over the years had much to worry about including noise, litter, carpet beating and problems created by people keeping horses and pigs.

To look after the Shelter and toilets there was also a caretaker and his wife, who were paid 24/- a week between them although this was soon raised to 28/-. This job clearly required tact, because in July 1914 the incumbents were sacked after 'complaints' had been received.

The careful and cautious attitude of the Council to every development and event concerning Penarth can be clearly seen in the abrupt refusal to the Cardiff Motor Club's request to hold races on the Esplanade in Easter 1914. There must also have been some concern for the safety of bathers because in July 1914 six lifebuoys and rescue poles were erected on the Esplanade.

Two contrasting views of the front before and after the construction of the block of shops in 1904. The top card is a pre-1902 printing with its other side restricted to the address.

Although much of the Windsor estate and the Council's activities seem to have been directed at the sea front and to encourage the 'better class' of visitor, both were conscious of their perceived view of the recreational needs of the local population. The continuing expansion of the town and the ever increasing numbers of visitors eventually persuaded the Town Council in 1899 to create public gardens for the towns folk and visitors. Luckily for them, Lord Windsor, who had now become the Lord Lieutenant of the County of Glamorgan, subsequently gave to the town the land on which Alexandra Park, Cliff Walk, Penarth Head Open Space, Arcot Street Shrubbery and the Plassey Street Recreation Ground were to be laid out. The first three of these were basically sea front developments which complemented those of the Windsor estate.

Alexandra Park

This park was laid out on an open field, bounded by two wooded dingles, overlooking the pier and the sea. The town was very fortunate because this could have been a prime building site for exclusive houses. Development quickly took place with paths laid and a shelter and bandstand constructed on newly cut terraces. Some of the earlier photographs show the park as a rather uninviting place with bare stone walls around the terraces, some young trees and shrubs, and a few flower beds. The planting was, however, well thought out and there is now a pleasant mix of conifers, hardwood trees, shrubs and open spaces with visual breaks and focal points. The stone walls are now almost completely hidden by a luxuriant growth of cotoneasters. The Park has steadily evolved and changed over the years although some trees such as the birch, near the aviary, appear to be part of the original plantings. The topiary, especially the yew birds near the Rectory Road entrance, are also features that are happily still there to be enjoyed.

Electric lighting was installed in the park by Edwards & Armstrong of Woking Street, Cardiff for £26.3s.3d, giving 12 lamps in the shelter and 48 in the bandstand. The total cost of the work for the park, together with the contracts for Cliff Walk and Plassey Street came to £4,741. 17s. 2d. The Park Lodge at the seaward end of the park, near the foot of Beach Hill, was built by John Jones for the sum of £658 for the Park Superintendent. A fashionable Monkey-puzzle tree was planted in its front garden which is now the best one in Penarth and regularly produces cones which show it to be female. The greenhouse just above Park Lodge were built at the same time as the house.

A Park Ranger, Mr Alexander Hall, was appointed at a wage of 7/- a week with a supplied uniform. An agreement was also reached with Mr Broadhurst for supplying music in the park on weekdays from June 23rd to September 23rd with the use of the bandstand and chairs. He was permitted to charge 1d for the use of the chairs and given the right to sell programmes.

A plan of Alexandra Gardens showing the proposed early layout of the paths and beds. The old route of Beach Road curves around to the Park entrance (Vale of Glamorgan).

The park was officially opened on Wednesday June 25th 1902 by the Chairman of the District Council, Mr. Samuel Thomas J.P. This was the day planned for the Coronation of Edward VII and the park, like so many others, was to be named after his wife Alexandra, the daughter of the Danish King. Unfortunately, Edward underwent an emergency operation for appendicitis and the Coronation was postponed until August 9th.

Nevertheless the Council had already taken the decision to proceed, so official opening of the park went ahead like countless other events around the country. It was a very grand affair. At 2 o'clock Members of the Council walked from the offices to the gates where the Chairman of the Park Committee - Mr Guy, the surveyor and the contractor's agent handed the key to Mr Thomas. The Council members and local dignitaries then toured the park. This was followed by speeches and the Yeomanry Band played in the new bandstand. The real Coronation day was marked by a 50 ft high bonfire on high ground near St Augustine's church.

Later that year, on Friday September 5th, Lord Windsor was received in the Council Offices and accompanied the Councillors by horse and carriage to the various plots of land that he had given to the town. Poles and bunting were erected and Mr Paul Draper's Band engaged to play between 4 and 8pm. The visit finished at Alexandra Park where Lord Windsor handed over the deeds of the various pieces of land he had given to the town. An address, prepared by the Council and illuminated at a cost of 15 guineas, was read and handed to Lord Windsor. This was accompanied by an album in scarlet morocco illustrated with coloured views of Penarth. Members of the Council and officials then entertained Lord Windsor to tea.

The bandstand, shelter and early topiary.

The view across Alexandra Park towards the houses in Beach Road.

Looking after baby near the cannon. A pre-1909 photograph because there is no pavilion on the pier.

Two views after the winter snows in January 1909. The upper shows houses in Bridgeman Road; the lower shows the Keeper's Cottage.

The Council must have thought the Park a success, for soon after it was opened a further 150 chairs were purchased. The Parks Committee then accepted a report recommending the expenditure of £210 on making two additional paths, erecting a rockery, placing netting to protect some of the greens and extending the area around the bandstand. Then recommended a further £80 be spent on steps up to the bandstand terrace and stepping other paths in brick. Two cannon from the Crimean War were placed just above the shelter to overlook the Bristol Channel.

The benches scattered throughout the park soon became popular places to sit and listen to the concerts that were regularly given in the bandstand. However, it should not be thought that everyone appreciated the park. Mr. Brain, the owner of Brain's Brewery in Cardiff, had recently purchased the nearby Pyke-Thomson's house Redlands in Plymouth Road and renamed it Roxburgh. A few months after the opening he complained to the Council about the miserable condition of the park and suggested, quite incorrectly, that there was no one to look after it. He also suggested that having bands was the cause of the problem and that they should be stopped, especially as local householders were complaining about the noise. He was clearly not alone in his worries because in September a proposal was put to the Parks Committee to enrol Honorary Junior Park Rangers to assist the Park Ranger. The Parks Committee did not follow up this suggestion, but recommended that the park should close earlier, at 7.30, in September and April, to reduce the night time noise - the original agreement was for the park to close 1¼ hours after sunset. Happily the complaints did not bring the musical events to an end and both bands and promenade concerts continued to be regular summertime attractions in the Park.

The Council did, however, introduce its own bye-laws in January 1903 to cover the Alexandra Park, Cliff Walk, Plassey Street Recreation Ground and Penarth Head View. The opening hours for Alexandra Park were set at 7am - 9.30pm May to August, 7am - 7.30pm April and September, 8am - 7pm March and October, and 8am - 5pm November to February. The byelaws also spelt out in detail many constraints on the use of the four public areas and threatened a punitive fine of £5 for anyone breaking them.

In 1907 an unexpected gift of New Zealand plants arrived from Mr J Guy, a former resident of Penarth, who thought that they might be acclimatised in the park. Unfortunately, it is not known if any of them survived for any length of time. Then in 1911 the Bristol Zoological Society gave the town an eagle which lived for many years in a cage situated in the park.

The park was sometimes used for official occasions as on May 21st 1910 when, at 4.30, the chairman of the Council read the proclamation of the accession of his Majesty King George V.

INDEX TO BYE-LAWS.

No.

1. Interpretation of terms.
2. Hours of opening and closing.
3. Unauthorised persons not to enter at other times.
4. Persons must enter and quit by the proper gates.
5. Persons shall not remove or deface notice boards.
6. Persons shall not damage fences, buildings, etc.
7. Persons shall not remove railings, seats, etc.
8. Persons shall not cause any beast of burden to enter.
9. Persons shall not cause any cow, sheep, pigs, etc., to enter.
10. Persons shall not bring any barrow, truck, etc., into
11. Persons shall not cause any damage with chaise or cycle.
,, The Council may prohibit same from certain parts.
12. Persons shall not post or affix any bill.
13. Persons shall not remove or disturb any soil.
14. Persons shall not walk over any flower bed, etc.
15. Persons shall not cut or remove turf, &c.
16. Persons shall not pluck any flower, etc.
17. Persons shall not defile any part or throw rubbish, etc., therein.
18. Persons shall not throw or discharge any missile.
19. Persons shall not climb any tree, barrier, etc.
20. Persons shall not wash in any ornamental water, or disturb any fish or fowl therein.
21. Persons shall not disturb any birds' nest.
22. Persons shall not snare or injure any bird.
23. Persons shall not cause any dog to enter without a leash, nor allow it to disturb or worry any animal or fowl.
24. Persons shall not erect any poles, tents, &c., without permission.
25. Persons shall not beat or cleanse any carpets, etc.
26. Persons shall not deposit any linen to dry or bleach.
27. Persons shall not deliver any public address except by permission.
28. Persons shall not play any musical instrument, or sing, except by permission.
29. Persons shall not sell or offer for sale.
30. Persons shall not disturb or annoy any person or any officer of the Council.
31. Persons shall not use obscene language, nor distribute bills.
32. Persons shall not frequent for the purpose of betting.
33. Penalty for breach of any of these Bye-laws, £5.
34. Persons may be removed for any breach of Bye-laws.
    I.—If name be unknown and cannot be ascertained.
    II.—If by remaining it appear likely another breach may be caused.
35. Nothing in these Bye-laws shall prejudice any right legally exercisable by persons over the Pleasure Grounds.

The Index to the 1903 Byelaws for parks and open spaces (Glamorgan County Records).

This, so-called, view of Alexandra Park is mainly of the Esplanade Hotel garden (post-marked 1912).

A view towards the pier with its pavilion. The bandstand is to the right and the fishpond to the left.

Cliff Walk

This walk was originally developed by the Windsor Estate on cliff top land running south from Cliff Road to a small copse of tress called the Seven Sisters (just beyond today's Stanton Way). It was taken over by the Local Board in 1886 as a public highway. It was improved in 1901 with the contractor being a Mr Thackery.

The Cliff top has always been an area for leisurely sport and a popular place to walk, especially as a rough footpath enables the more energetic to continue further along the cliff to Lavernock. Unfortunately, erosion has always been a major problem because the cliff is so unstable that the edge has been known to recede up to one foot in a year. A gate to an older path can now be seen near the edge of the cliff at the Cliff Road entrance.

Penarth Head Open Space

This headland has probably been the most difficult public space to manage and develop. Part of the headland was offered to the town in 1899 by Lord Windsor. However, because the Government was expressing interest in this land for the purpose of constructing a fort to protect Cardiff and Penarth Docks, Lord Windsor offered instead the adjacent piece of land to the south. The Council accepted and, being the highest point is south Glamorgan, it gave visitors spectacular views over the beach and the Bristol Channel. The worried Council did, however, write to the Government urging them not to build a fort on the headland, because of potential structural damage to property if the guns were fired. In 1902, Lord Windsor added to this space by giving the council the adjacent piece of land formerly owned by Lloyd's' Shipping Agency as a look-out and signal station. The station itself and some sheds that stood on the land had originally cost £105 to construct, but these were offered to the Council and bought for only £50.

A spate of stone throwing from the top caused the Council to erect railings at a cost of £45 and to consider closing the area at night.

The open Headland was an excellent viewpoint to watch ships come and go from both Penarth and Cardiff Docks. On the 15th June 1910 it was crowded to capacity, as were the pier and esplanade, to watch the Terra Nova leave Cardiff Docks on Captain Scott's ill-fated attempt to reach the South Pole.

THE SECOND PHASE OF DEVELOPMENT 1911 - 1939

The Council were just starting to make several improvements to the Esplanade area when war broke out in Europe. Six seats were installed in 1914, but then all developments went on hold. For a while the war had no real impact upon Penarth itself and everyone was convinced that it would be over within a few months. But, as the war dragged on and the stalemate of trench warfare continued, thoughts turned to defending the coastline. The Government had plans to build a coastal battery on Penarth headland to protect Penarth and Cardiff Docks and two guns were soon positioned here. Large gangs of men were employed to cut away the top of the cliff so that the guns could be trained on the narrow entrance to Cardiff docks. The pier was requisitioned by the army for use as a searchlight post, but the lights were subsequently moved in 1917 to specially built platforms under Penarth Head that were accessed by steps from the cliff top. There were also barbed-wire defences at the north end of the beach beneath the Kymin and a submarine net protected the Docks.

Even with the army in charge of the pier the public still had limited access. Although there were a few shows in the pavilion, virtually all the paddle steamers had been requisitioned for use as mine sweepers. The only steamer left was the Duchess of Devonshire which maintained a limited service between Cardiff and Weston.

Penarth Head with the search-light towers. The Kymin is in the left foreground.

It is, perhaps, interesting to reflect at this point on the changing fortunes of the two original premier shipping families in Penarth. The Morel Brothers, who came from the Channel Islands and J. Cory and Sons who came from Padstow were the top two in the league of local ship owners having, in 1884, fleets of 26 ships (36,757 total gross tonnage) and 17 ships (23,641 total gross tonnage) respectively. The number of ships registered in the South Wales ports gradually increased so that by 1904 there were 150 at Cardiff, 20 at Penarth, 58 at Barry, 24 at Port Talbot and 98 at Swansea. By 1914 the Morel Brothers had slipped to number 9 in the league with 10 ships (25,154 total gross tonnage) and J.Cory and Sons to number 3 even though they had increased their fleet to 19 ships (54,308 total gross tonnage). The new, locally connected, Evan Thomas, Radcliffe and Company were the new leaders with 28 ships (114,649 total gross tonnage).

An early aerial view of Penarth and the Docks from the north. St Augustine's Church is top right with Penarth Hotel, Undercliff, Northcliff and The Ferns to the left (Penarth Times).

To compound the towns problems, Britain as a whole fell into a state of great economic depression in the 1920s. Many companies went into liquidation and vast numbers of people were out of work. The depression followed a boom in both dock and ship building so now there were too many docks and too many ships chasing diminishing amounts of cargo. The effect was particularly marked in South Wales where the docks were heavily dependent on exports of coal and imports of iron ore, pitwood and Black Sea grain. Coal exports were down as well because the British Navy had changed over to oil-fired boilers in all their ships.

In Penarth several prominent residents such as Sir Sven Hansen, owner of the Hansen Shipping Line, and Mr A.G. Harrison, Chairman of the Town Shipping Line, were virtually bankrupted by the collapse of their shipping empires. The Hansens left Penarth and their house at the Paddocks was sold.

OPENING DATES OF DOCKS AND HARBOURS IN SOUTH WALES

1798	Cardiff - The Glamorganshire Canal Sea Lock.
1837	Aberavan Dock
1842	Newport - Town Dock
1843/9	Cardiff Bute West Dock
1845	Neath Harbour improvements
1852	Swansea North Dock
1855/9	Cardiff Bute East Dock
1859	**Penarth Ely Harbour** Swansea - South Dock
1861	Briton Ferry Dock
1865	**Penarth Dock**
1867	Porthcawl Dock
1874	Cardiff Roarth Dock
1875	Newport - Alexandra South Dock
1877	Neath Harbour
1881	Swansea Prince of Wales Dock
1884	**Penarth Dock extension**
1887	Cardiff Roath Dock
1889	Barry No. 1 Dock
1893/1914	Newport - Alexandra South Dock extension
1898	Barry No. 2 Dock Swansea Prince of Wales Dock extension Port Talbot Dock
1907	Cardiff Queen Alexandra Dock
1909	Swansea King's Dock

After hostilities ceased, the town tried to get back to its original position as a leading seaside town of class, but there was one major problem. The Pier had fallen into disrepair while it was in the hands of the army and, because the Pier Company failed to get adequate post war compensation for repair, they let it fall into near ruin. Although the pier and the pavilion were soon open as usual, the wooden landing stage had deteriorated to such an extent that it was unusable for steamers. The Pier Company had received virtually no income since the start of the war and the steamers did not return from mine sweeping until 1919. The owners were not in a financial position to undertake the necessary work. Penarth was without one of its major visitor attractions and local business people expressed concern.

After a number of Council debates and much argument in the local press, the Council entered into an agreement to purchase the Pier in 1923. In August, the Council's offer of £5,000 was accepted by the Pier Company, but events moved very slowly until the Provisional Order to purchase the pier was received in July 1924 and permission was also given to widen the landward end of the pier. The Parliamentary Bill approving this did not receive Royal Assent until August 1st 1924. The Pier was purchased in October that year and the Council decided to press ahead with its restoration and developing the Promenade because visitors were deserting the town for other local coastal spots. In 1923, even St Mary's Well Bay (often disparagingly referred to as bare bottom bay) had more visitors than Penarth.

In an attempt to get people back to work, the Government introduced a scheme of grants which enabled worthy public works to be largely centrally funded. Many seaside towns undertook some rather bold development plans through such money and Penarth was no exception. Changes in local government in 1924 had created Penarth Urban District Council which, like many other sea-side towns, decided to initiate several schemes to improve the sea-front. These were to involve the Pier, Beach Road, the Italian Gardens and the Promenade and together were to be the last of the major formal developments to promote leisure and elegance in the town.

The first major new work undertaken by the Council in 1924 was to alter the curve at the bottom of Beach Road to its present route thereby making the approach to the Esplanade easier. Even so, many reports in the *Penarth Times* reveal that cyclists continued to have accidents on this hill; there was one fatality and many others had to seek hospital treatment for broken bones. The wider route of the new road constructed through the land of the Kymin left an isolated block of land which remained undeveloped for many years. The Seabank block of flats is there now.

Eventually work began on the pier in December 1924 by Messrs Noel Brodie of Bristol who rebuilt the old wooden landing stage in concrete, and restored decking and foundations for £10,000. It is interesting to reflect on the wages that workmen were earning at that time. The Foreman Carpenter working on the decking was paid 14s 2d an hour which was an enormous amount as he did not work very many hours on the project. Carpenters and painters were paid 1s 4d an hour, scaffolders 1s 3½d and labourers 1s 2d.

In anticipation of the Pavilion's reopening, actors were booked and lists of the shows were available by March. When the Pier opened in April 1926 new bylaws were issued and pier charges introduced with prices set at:

Persons promenading 1d
Single tickets for passengers landing or embarking 3d
Return tickets for passengers landing and embarking 5d
Luggage large and small 2d a packet
Fishing ticket including admission 6d.

On Easter Wednesday, the Chairman of the Council, Chas. P. Deverall, opened the pier and the Glen Avon arrived to take a specially invited party for a cruise to Weston-super-Mare. A gun salute was fired from the Yacht Club which was answered by the Glen Avon's siren. The party had luncheon on board and returned at 2pm. A limited service then operated until May after which Campbell's steamers entered into a regular service. Boat trips were clearly popular with 200 passengers being recorded on one boat to Weston-super Mare and 100 on a trip to Bristol. It was not all one way traffic from Penarth, because many visitors were once again returning to the town in steadily increasing numbers.

Councillor and Mrs Deverall opening the Pier's landing stage (Penarth News).

The Promenade and Pier Pavilion were popular venues attracting many visitors. The Council, however, had grander plans for both. The Promenade was widened with money supplied by the Government through its Unemployment Grants Scheme. The original Promenade was increased by 21 feet to its present width of 60 feet, although it was only increased in height by a fraction of an inch. It was constructed of reinforced concrete and designed with an arched face and rounded coping to curve the waves back onto themselves. Even this construction is, however, insufficient to prevent flooding by extremely high tides. Perhaps the worst occasion was in October 1945 when the combination of spring tides and a gale flooded the shops and made the road impassable every tide for two days. Pedestrians were now protected by stout railings and access to the beach was made possible by specially made non-slip concrete steps in the two semicircular bastions that jut out 25 feet. The construction was completed by Messrs Francis Joseph Thomas of Peare Street, Cardiff in 15 months by starting work at both ends. The total cost was £22,974 13s. 0d. of which the Unemployment Grants Committee agreed to give 75% of the total amount.

The work on the promenade was not without its own rather peculiar problem. This was what the press referred to as 'The Great Smell' which pervaded the front for most of the summer months in 1926. Seaweed had been washed up by the high tides to become lodged between the old wall and the new wall being constructed. Here it had rotted. The Council tried, unsuccessfully, to get the contractor to clear the seaweed and by October the Councillors' patience ran out and they resorted to the Courts. At Court Mr Edgar Evans, the Town Surveyor, said that in his opinion seaweed had rotted in water and been trodden in until it had become a black filthy mass which smelt rather like rotten eggs and revealed maggots and an advanced stage of decomposition when cut. Mr Foster of the Gwalia Restaurant informed the Court that his property was right on the spot with the result that he obtained full benefit of the smell. His trade had suffered considerably in consequence and he added that 'people who arrived ran back with their noses tightly enveloped in handkerchiefs'. Howard Leonard, the Piermaster, testified that the smell had continued since April or May and described it as 'Horrible, really indescribable.' The Contractor had earlier argued that the smell came from horse dung washed onto the beach, but clearly thought better of trying that line of defence in Court. Instead, he argued that there was no nuisance and that the smell present was a smell which had existed on the beach for many years. He also claimed that the contractors were neither owners nor occupiers of the site but licensees. The Council had given authority for the wall to be built and this wall was the cause of the alleged nuisance; therefore the Council were responsible. A nice try, but the Court found against him so he was instructed to clean out the offending seaweed. 'The Great Smell' came to an end to everyone's relief.

Workmen building the new Esplanade front wall (Penarth News).

The view from the beach along a partially completed section of the Esplanade. Work on the pier has not yet started (Penarth News).

Penarth Regatta seen from the Esplanade.

An interesting superimposition of two photographs to give a view of Penarth in a 'storm'.

Meanwhile another scheme was initiated on the front on the open rough ground to the south of the Beach Shelter. The inspiration for a garden on this site came from the first Lady Chairman of the Council (1924/25), Mrs Constance Maillard. She was also a pioneer in developing welfare schemes for mothers and children in the town. She lived to be 103 years old and a plaque to commemorate her was placed in the back wall of the garden in 1988. Miss Ursula Thompson had discussed the idea of the garden with Mrs Maillard when she was on holiday at her home in Park Road. Ursula Thompson was the first woman to graduate as a gardener from Kew Gardens, but was forced to go to Italy to find work. It was from her work in restoring Italian gardens that her ideas for the new sea front garden came. She drew up a number of plans and lists of plants for Mrs Maillard who subsequently took some of the Council Members to visit Mr Evers' Rock Garden at Llanishen to see what might be suitable for Penarth. The visit must have been a success for the new garden was constructed and opened in March 1926 as part of the seaside development. It was first described as the Beach Rock Gardens, the New Rock Garden, or the Promenade Garden, but later became known as the Italian Garden presumably because of its formal terraced layout. The opening of the garden was, as usual, a grand affair attended by most of the Councillors and their wives. The Chairman of the Council, C.P.Deverall accepted a golden key from the Surveyor, Edgar Evans, and then gave a speech to the assembled large crowd. In it he thanked Mr Wilfed Evers for designing them, Mr Edgar Evans for laying them out and Mr Rees James, the Park Superintendent, for carry out the designs. He then went on to extol the beauty of Penarth adding that it was already known throughout the length and breadth of the land as the most beautiful little town in Wales. Councillor Jones also recalled happy memories of when he opened the Public Shelter twenty three years earlier and remembered the time when the tide used to beat against the hedge which grew where the esplanade now stood. The party then went into the shelter where they were guests of Mr Deverall for a 'sumptuous tea'.

Interestingly, no mention was made of Mrs Maillard, Ursula Thompson nor Bryn Price, the Park Keeper, whose men had themselves cut back the cliff and had to move the stone in wheel barrows because it was too dangerous to use horses.

The view from the roof of the shelter across the Esplanade Garden towards Sea Cot and the new Esplanade.

A later photograph of the steps in the garden. See how much the trees have grown.

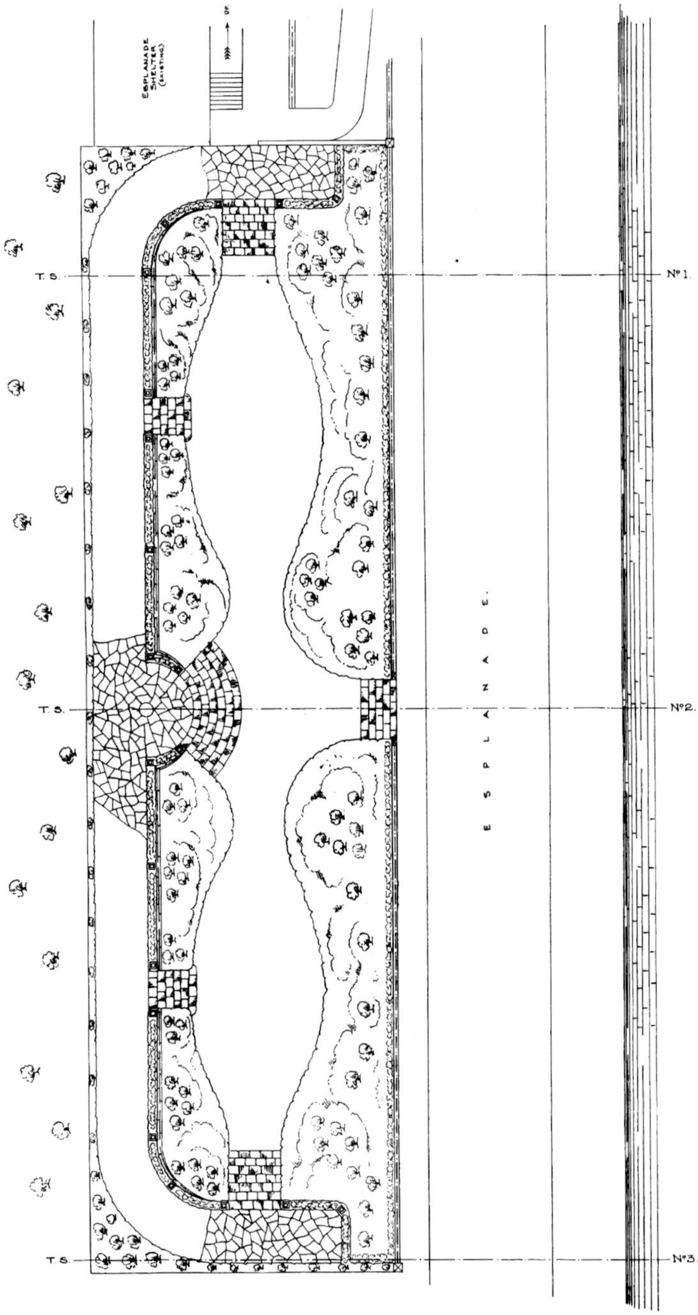

The plan for the 'New Rock Garden' (Vale of Glamorgan).

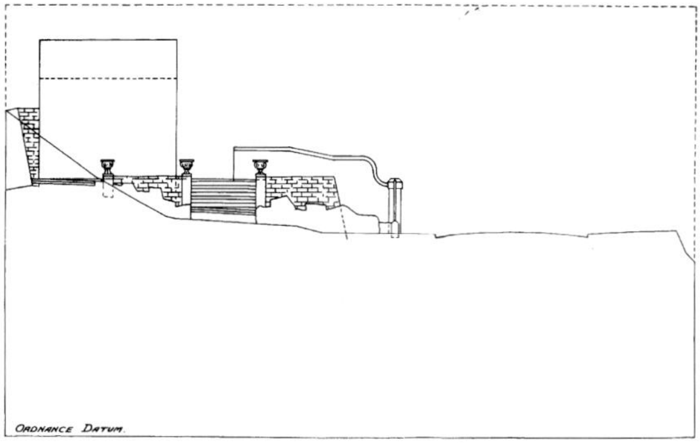

—TRANSVERSE SECTION Nº 1.—

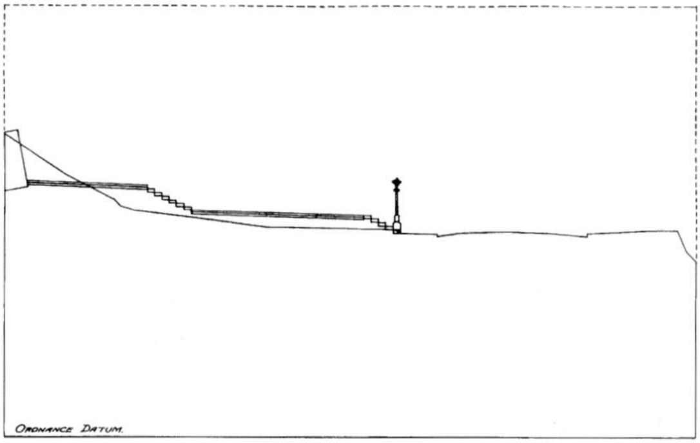

—TRANSVERSE SECTION Nº 2.—

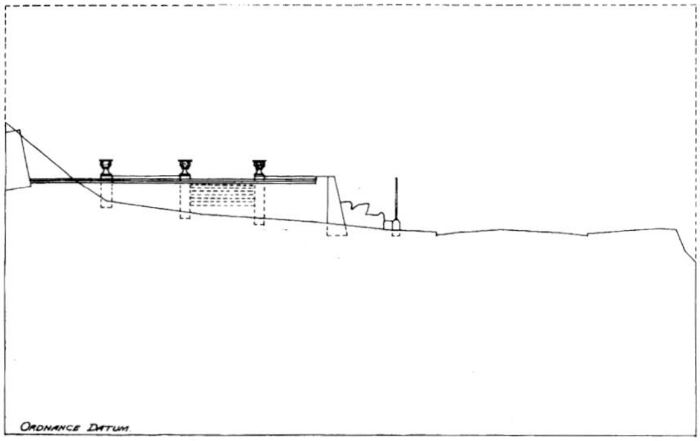

—TRANSVERSE SECTION Nº 3.—

— EDGAR. I. EVANS. ASSOC. M. INST. C. E. —
— CHARTERED CIVIL ENGINEER. —
— PENARTH. —
— AUGUST 1924. —

Councillor and Mrs Deverall at the opening of the 'Esplanade Gardens' (Penarth News).

Laying the foundation stone for the Pier (Penarth News).

The Council's plans for the Pier involved widening the landward end for the construction of a new Pavilion and shops and the Council Surveyor recommended advertising for tenders about the end of May 1926. Unfortunately, their application for a government grant towards its cost was turned down which led to many comments in the local press about the burden on the local rate payers. Nevertheless, the Council decided to go ahead, but immediately encountered problems. The work on the new Promenade was restricting access to the Pier and prevented the contractor from having a suitable storage area. In August the chaotic state of the Promenade even caused the operating Pier Pavilion to close. The considerable delay in starting work on the pier, coupled by the rising prices of cement (up to 10/- a ton) and iron (up by 10-15%), eventually caused the contractor, Mr McColville of Abergavenny, to refuse the contract. The next two contractors on the list refused for the same reason. Finally in January 1927 the Yorkshire Herribique Concrete Company was contracted to carry out the work for £5449 (only £149 more than had been agreed with Mr McColville) with the stipulation that some of the local 1,000 unemployed men were taken on. The work was soon underway with the foundation stone being laid on the site by Mr Stanley Smith J.P. in April. The Earl of Plymouth was there at the time. The construction work was clearly of wider interest as well because the ëPenarth Pier and Landing Stage' was featured in the *Ferro-Concrete Review* that year.

Thoughts turned to the beach with suggestions for bathing boxes, which were not purchased. There were new byelaws for the treatment of donkeys on the beach limiting their hours to 11-1, 2-5, 5.30-8. Then there were discussions about unfair competition from Cardiff boatmen who were allowed to operate at Penarth beach, while Penarth boatmen were prohibited in Cardiff. The *Penarth Times* also carried complaints about the poor condition of boats for hire on the beach.

Good boatman on the Esplanade,
You seem a decent man;
Now, couldn't that boat of yours be made
A little more spick and span?

Your chances surely are remote
For letting it out to hire
For he who wants to hire a boat
Wants one he can admire.

So if you want to make it pay,
Remove its shabby taint;
Give it at once, this very day,
A decent coat of paint.

Penarth Times

Work on the Promenade and the Pier was generally welcomed but, even though visitors still came in large numbers especially on the Bank Holidays, it had an overall very bad effect on trade during 1927. In fact on August Bank Holiday 1927 an estimated 6-7,000 visitors came to Penarth leading to crowding on the Promenade and its new garden, the Pier and the Cliff Walk. Work on the Pier and Promenade meant that the seats had not yet been put back and the few available deck chairs had been soon snapped up at 2d each. That year the Great Western Railway (G.W.R.) carried about 500,000 passengers from Cardiff to Penarth, exclusive of the great number of season ticket holders. The increasing popularity of Penarth led the G.W.R. to issue tourist tickets in 1928 to the town from all over the country. The larger numbers of visitors prompted the Council to appoint a Beach Inspector for the summer season. The wages were set at £2.3s.0d a week and he was supplied with a blue serge suit and mackintosh.

An additional effect of all these developments was that the Promenade was becoming an all year round attraction, so there were soon requests for the shelter to remain open in winter.

Nevertheless, the beach itself was not a very popular place at this time and was much emptier than the crowded sands of Whitmore Bay on Barry Island. Penarth's residents tended to ignore Barry Island as vulgar and brash, but they could not so easily ignore the nearby St Mary's Well Bay. Some people did walk along the cliffs to the beach there, but the vast majority came from Cardiff by train. The prejudiced thoughts of the more refined Penarth residents were reflected in an unsigned article that appeared in the *Penarth Times* in September 1926. The writer was clearly appalled by what he saw when on his visit. After attempting to drink an awful cup of tea, observing 'the great undressed from Grangetown' being confronted with 'three painted young ladies' changing right in front of him and disturbing a 'card school,' he left the beach disgusted and struggled up what he saw as a dangerous slippery path. He concluded with:

'From the road I glanced down and saw before me a well filled fly-paper, a bobbing, common, bawling mass of humanity joined together. Not a vestige of decency; morals swept by the board. Terrible sanitary arrangements; what accommodation is provided does not cope with the demands, and the undergrowth stinks with excrescence.

Although our District Council roll their eyes on the mention of mixed bathing, they sit complacently quiet and let this kind of thing go on next door; allow all those precious lives to be jeopardised by rocks which are constantly falling, a path that is a death trap, and arrangements which are a crime. Is it any wonder that the once beautiful pleasure resort of the decent has degenerated into a hole of vice and gambling?'

Penarth beach and St Mary's Well Bay were certainly worlds apart.

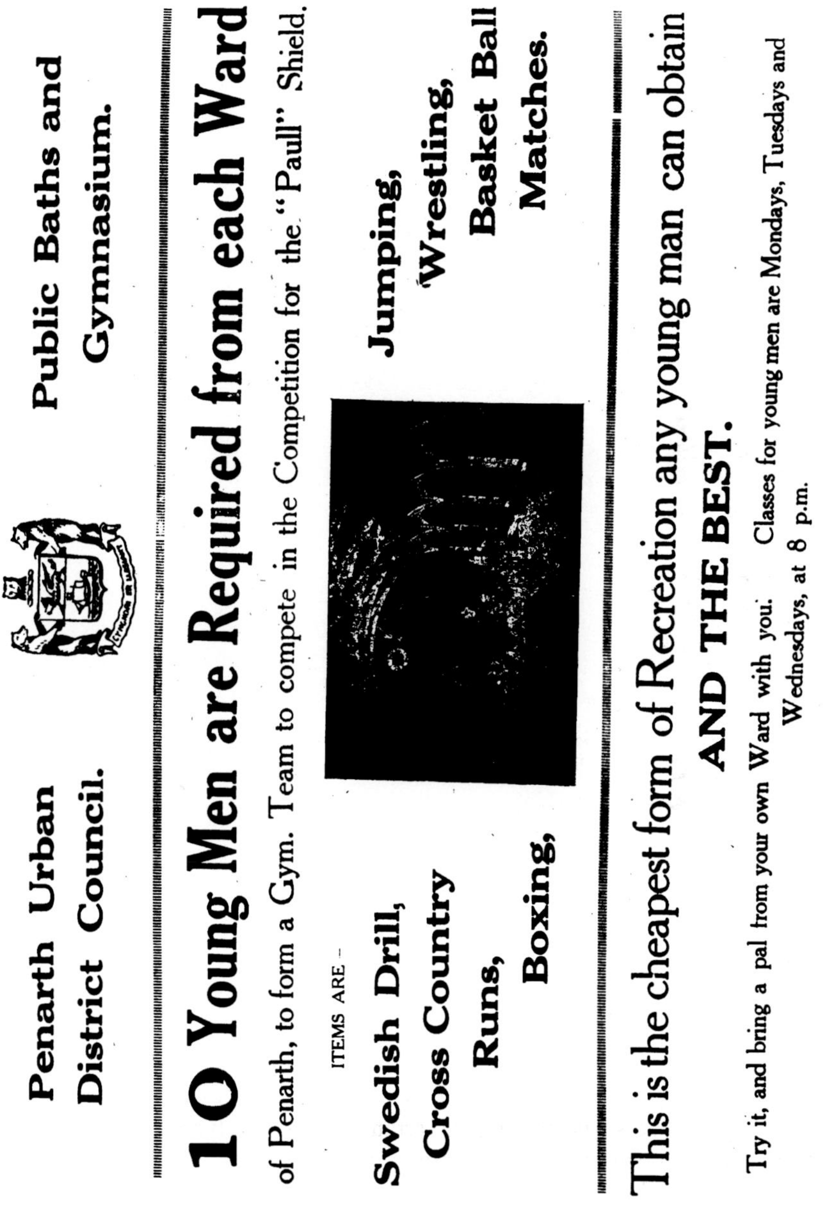

An advertisement in the Penarth Times (1926).

The pier during the landward reconstruction. The temporary ticket office is on the decking near the shelters.

Discussion continued in the Council about proposals for the development of the enlarged pier and it was eventually agreed to proceed with the erection of a Pier Pavilion at an estimated cost of £8,000 and its fitting out for a further £2,000. The plans for the new concrete pavilion were first submitted to the Board of Trade in 1926. The Council believed that the income from the Pavilion would pay for the necessary loan, although the press revealed that there was some public disquiet about the matter and that people did not want another 'box of bricks'. The *Penarth Times* also noted at this time that London newspapers were asserting that there was immodesty on the beach as bathers were using mackintoshes and umbrellas as shelters and that even these were often put aside.

In October 1927 tenders were received for the Pavilion and Alderman Samuel Thomas and Mr Edgar Evans went to London to interview the Minister to get the necessary loan. It was optimistically estimated that the work would commence in April and last six months. The Penarth Chamber of Commerce was against the building of the Pavilion, arguing that the cost was too great because the total cost of the Pier and Esplanade would be £52,000 and that after 15 years of possible Government grants the entire cost would have to be borne by ratepayers. Nevertheless, work on the Pavilion went ahead with a bold new Art Deco design, by a Mr Somerset, and a projected seating capacity of 600. The contract went to a Mr E.J.Smith of Cardiff for his price of £9,000, but work did not progress as fast as expected. The framework was up by February the next year but the Pavilion was nowhere near finished when the Pier was opened for shipping on April 4th. That year P & A Campbell was charged £75 for the use of

Miss Kathleen Thomas on her triumphal return to Penarth Pier being the first person to swim across the Bristol Channel. She actually swam 25 miles, in 7 hours 20minutes, on her route from Penarth to Weston-super-Mare. The distance is only 12½ miles but the tidal flow in the channel can carry swimmers miles off course so careful planning of time of departure is vital. Twenty year old Kathleen had been girls champion more than once, had become Welsh lady championship swimmer at the annual gala at Penarth Baths, and was a popular member of Penarth Swimming Club for many years. She was, therefore, well known and perfect for a local heroine.
(Penath Times).

the Pier, which was a 50% increase over 1927. Nevertheless, it was a good season for sailing, with large numbers of passengers taking advantage of the Paddle-Steamers. Meanwhile, the Council asked the Penarth Electric Lighting Company and the Cardiff Gas Company to tender for lighting the Promenade and the Pier and then accepted their Lighting Committee's recommendation to use electricity.

In 1928 the Esplanade was ready for the official opening on Empire Day, May 24th. The seats were even back in position near the new railings. For this occasion, the Pier, Yacht Club and other sea front buildings were decorated with flags and the traditional white ribbon was cut in front of the public shelter by Councillor Frank Humphries. Afterwards, in the Rock Garden, the local cross-channel swimmer, Miss Kathleen Thomas, was presented a silver tea service. Miss Doris Pawley sang Elgar's Land of Hope and Glory and the Abercynon Silver Prize Band entertained the large crowd who had come to watch. Meanwhile three elaborately decorated buses owned by Messrs. White Ltd, South Wales Commercial Motors and Cardiff Corporation paraded on the Esplanade. These three companies had all been recently given permission to run services down Beach Hill to the Esplanade although their speed was limited to 5 mph on the hill and 10 mph on the Esplanade.

Penarth was clearly becoming widely know. In March 1928 a deck chair proprietor in the Isle of Man wrote to the Council seeking permission to place seats on the sand. It is not recorded what the actual reply was, but the suggestion was greeted with laughter by Council Members who suggested the proprietor should also bring the sand with him from the Isle of Man.

Councillor Frank Humphries cutting the tape in connection with the re-opening of the esplanade.

The town's presentation of a silver tea service to Miss Kathleen Thomas by Councillor Frank Humphries, in connection with her notable Bristol Channel swim.

Two views of the new Esplanade (the upper one is post-marked 1928).

Penarth was now becoming a popular place for events and 1928 seemed to be a particularly good year for them. In early June two destroyers, HMS Velox and HMS Walker, paid a courtesy visit to Penarth Dock. There was a civic reception for the officers, who were than driven around the town to see all the places of interest. The several thousand crew were given free entry to the pier and the Baths and the manager of the Windsor Kinema offered them free shows. The ships were open to the public at the weekend attracting large crowds of sightseers. The Council members were entertained to tea on board before the ships departed for Cornwall.

On the morning of June 14th an estimated 50,000 people were on the front to welcome Sir Alan Cobham in his Flying Boat. There were 500 cars parked in the vicinity of the Pier and a record 2,500 people were on the Pier, with many of them going down onto the lower deck of the landing stage. At 10.30 Cobham circled low twice, but the sea was too rough to land and he was forced to land in smoother water in Cardiff bay near Penarth Head. People rushed through the Kymin and Church Avenue to get a closer look. Then, at 3 pm, Cobham took off again and flew over the Esplanade on his way to Southampton.

Later that month, Princess Mary was a guest of the Lord Lieutenant, the Earl of Plymouth, at St Fagans Castle. She visited Penarth to meet the senior Council Members and see the front and the Rock Garden while on her way to lay the foundation stone for the new Llandough hospital.

Bristol Channel swimming was also always a serious affair and drew large crowds to watch. Even the start of an attempted swim to Weston-super-Mare at 1.30 a.m. on a Sunday morning in June brought 150 sightseers. Then in August the crowds were there again to watch two people, Edith Parnell and Dennis Tidbath (both 15 years old) swim from Flat Holm to Penarth. This took 4$^{1}/_{2}$ hours during which time the ebb tidal race off Sully Island prevented them from making any headway for almost half-an-hour. Next year Edith ParnelΔ101

1 swam the Bristol Channel from Penarth to Weston-super-Mare in 10 hours 17 minutes. A considerable ordeal considering the tide took her to opposite Barry Harbour forcing her to swim between Flat Holme and Steep holme. When Miss Elsie Westarborg became the centre of a dispute over receiving massage for cramp during her August crossing, passionate debate ensued over the rights or wrongs of the Welsh Amateur Swimming Association's decision not to award the certificate.

Surprisingly, it was not until 1970 that someone swam the Channel both ways. It was in August that year that Mr Bill Pickering, described by the press as a 17 stone vegetarian, came ashore south of Penarth thereby missing much of the welcome that had been organised for him.

It should be remembered that large numbers of Penarth's residents were out of work and any event was worth watching to kill time. In September 1928 there were 1,000 unemployed (with dependants totalling 5,000 out of a population of 19,000) who sent deputations to the Council asking for work on roads, paths and other potential developments. Captain Arthur Evans MP addressed over 600 of

Crowds on the newly finished Esplanade in 1928. The new Beach Road route is visible straight ahead. The new Pavilion is under construction on the Pier on the right.

A closer view of Beach Road in 1928. The iron work of the new pavilion and shops can be seen on the right.

the unemployed at a meeting at the Hippodrome where he talked about national and local aspects of large scale unemployment. Door to door begging started and a Penarth Santa Claus (for children's presents) and Distress Fund was set up.

Worse was still to come when the Great Western Railway Company closed the Penarth Dock locomotive shed in April 1929. Another 140 men were out of work with a loss of £400-£500 weekly to the town's economy. Eventually in 1936 even the Docks themselves closed.

One of the few good personal things to emerge from all this was the Penarth Ladies Choir which was formed in 1926 as a basis for aiding the Penarth Distress Fund. The choir gained such popularity that it carried on after the emergency was over and won first prize at the National Eisteddfod at Wrexham at the first competition they ever entered.

The numbers of visitors to Penarth steadily increased and attracted much business interest. The increasing trade even prompted the Esplanade Hotel to open an Esplanade Hotel Café which advertised that everything was of the highest quality, e.g. nothing but Grade A milk was used and the cups, saucers and plates were of pure china. The visitors might have been coming and spending much needed money in the town, but the ever watchful Council continued to be very selective in what they permitted. Six weighing machines were allowed on the Esplanade and Pier but sweet machines were certainly not. The August Bank Holiday crowd in 1928 was huge, but was, however, seen as an invasion by many local people. The *Penarth Times* commented in its next issue 'These people may have created for one day a 'appy 'Amstead', but they have quite disappeared, and the more high-toned visitors will once again be left to enjoy Penarth's attractions, and the air of carnival, broad humour and easy merriment that marked the Bank Holiday will be but a memory.' Maybe this town attitude was reflected in some of the other decisions such as only opening the shelter toilets on the Esplanade for six months in the year. It makes you wonder if the town really wanted day visitors. I suspect a large number of residents did not.

The Council appeared to be accepting many changes that year. Mixed bathing in the Swimming Baths was finally allowed that summer after years of argument, but only after the construction of an extension for additional changing facilities. An extra assistant was also hired to superintend the conduct of the swimmers and to stop any undesirable 'horse-play'. Within a week the *Penarth Times* was reporting both an increase in the number of swimmers and of litter in the Bath changing rooms. That year it was also recognised that the age of the motor car was coming for the Council agreed to parking for 25-30 cars alongside the Esplanade Hotel at the entrance to Alexandra Park.

Work on the Pavilion was, however, proceeding very slowly. By November the *Penarth Times* was referring to the building of the Pavilion as a standing joke saying that it had been promised for August, then December and that now it might not be not ready for Easter 1929. The paper also called it an unattractive and expensive structure and suggested that the money might have been better spent elsewhere.

Planning for the Pavilion opening got underway in early 1929 as the pleas for completion continued. The delay was affecting long term trade because visitors had started going elsewhere to resorts, such as Barry, where there were plenty of facilities. It was suggested that the National Orchestra of Wales be booked for the opening, especially when the BBC took up the option of having a permanent line to the Pavilion. In March tenders were invited for seating, staging and lighting and a furious row brewed up because only outside firms were allowed to tender for the lighting. In April a lighting scheme was accepted for about £900 and Messrs Howell Ltd of Cardiff were employed to renovate the old Pavilion seats for £395 9s 5d. However, in April 1929 disaster nearly struck. The French sailing Vessel Brittonue was anchored off Penarth in bad weather when it was dragged to within 30 feet of the Pier. Only fast action by the coastguard and Cardiff tugs prevented severe damage to the Pier.

The attention of the whole town was on the opening of the Pavilion with many seeing it as the key to the town's revival as a premier resort.

Oh Sol, respect our hours of ease,
Be charming, kindly, if you please,
Be our staunch friend, the staunchest made,
We want no fires upon the hearth,
We want your smiles on fair Penarth.

Oh! Sol, your manners are so queer -
Sometimes they tend to disappear -
You take your smiles to other lands,
Leaving your frowns upon our hands,
Leaving us just the aftermath,
It isn't kind to fair Penarth.

Oh Sol, don't hide behind the clouds
And disappoint the surging crowds
Who'll come to gaze (we hope) upon
Our monster new pavilion!
We want. Oh! Sol, a sunshine bath
At Whitsuntide, in fair Penarth.

PRECELLY (*Penarth Times*)

The Pavilion was eventually opened on Saturday May 18th, 1929 by the Chairman of the Council, Mrs Pertwee M.B.E., J.P., even though the interior decorations were not yet finished. Mrs Pertwee opened the lock with a gold key declaring the building 'open for ever,' which was perhaps not very apt now looking back at its rather chequered history. Mrs Pertwee added that it was wonderful to see the building complete and that she would like to see lectures, reviews and concerts during the winter and also a series of Shakespearean plays. The whole Pier redevelopment scheme had by now cost about £30,000, but most of the town welcomed the Council's attempts to make the town so much more attractive to locals and visitors alike. The *Penarth Times* thought it a splendid building and very well built, writing 'surely the Pavilion has a life of 999 years so solidly built is it.' How wrong can you be!

The first public show at the Pavilion was a new and unusual song and dance review called the 'Lido Follies'. It was followed by a varied programme to which the public came in large numbers. Even so, the Pavilion was very rarely filled to capacity and, when the colder winter months came there were many complaints about the rather startling lack of heating. Lectures and Shakespeare plays seem to have been given a miss and there was even a ban on Sunday concerts.

Mrs. Pertwee accepting the Pavilion key (Penarth Times).

Two views of the new art deco Pier Pavilion soon after it opened. Constructed of reinforced concrete and always painted in pastel colours, its most recognisable art deco features are the topee-shaped domelets and the semi-circular 'Tuscan colonnaded entrance.

Penarth pier seen from Cliff Walk.

An aerial view of the newly completed pier, with both pavilions and the new esplanade. Alexandra Park and Windsor Gardens are both clearly visible as are the the old and new routes of Beach Road.

All was not yet perfect. The leaseholder of the Pavilion, Mr Alfred Newton, complained that the plush seating was not ready and that he was losing money. The Council were meanwhile debating whether the lease was for six or seven days a week and if free use should be allowed for charitable and national organisations. In June the Council decided to establish their rights to Sunday use of the Pavilion, much to the annoyance of Mr Newton.

A booking-acknowledgement card from the Esplanade Hotel (coloured red on the monochrome post card).

Public attention, meanwhile, had turned to the intolerable state of the Old Pavilion. Nevertheless, even though it was dirty and untidy, the overwhelming opinion was against pulling it down. Instead there was talk of installing a few plants and palms and an automatic piano and turning it into a pleasant shelter which would add to the Pier's income. After a series of meetings, £100 was spent on making good the building and surveying it to see if the floor could be made good for dancing. Finally it was agreed to approve a plan to refurbish the Pavilion for dancing, roller skating and as a shelter for steamer passengers. It would have involved a new roof, the enlargement of the vestibule and the addition of two impressive domes. An application was made to the Ministry for financial support to defray the estimated £1,138 costs. The application was turned down so a new simpler scheme was designed for reroofing and reflooring at a cost of approximately £500.

In late October 1929 a Penarth Resident, Mrs Esther Harris, donated a double-faced clock to be fitted on the front of the Pavilion with a plate in

The view from Penarth Head in 1929.

The paddling pool.

commemoration of her late husband, Hyman, and son, Solly who had died in the Great War. The Penarth Crest was on one side and a Jewish symbol on the other. Soon a few grumbles were being heard from the younger residents who had now lost their excuse of not knowing that it was time for them to be at home.

The Pier Pavilion with its new clock projecting from the semi-circular entrance.

THE PAVILION CLOCK
"Hickory Dickory Dock!"
"Who is there?"
"The Pavilion Clock."
No mouse would dare run up my face,
I'd send him off at a rattling pace,
I'd make him tremble through and through
If he should (while I'm marking time)
Copy that mouse in nursery rhyme.
No, No! Not So!
Not for me!
Here am I, the Pavilion Clock,
Taking stock of the crowds that flock
On the Esplanade
Below.
Nobody ever, in fair Penarth,
Will be late for tea anymore,
For I am here;
And I've come to cheer
You all the year
I'm yours, the Pavilion Clock.

PRECELLY (*Penarth Times*)

The Council was also experimenting with demonstrations of loud speakers on the Esplanade. The speakers naturally brought some adverse comments leading Precelly in the *Penarth Times* to write:

Try for ever, you will never
Hope to please the people (all);
You may strive, you may endeavour,
with your backs against the wall.

Speakers (loud) that all may hear,
Some would like upon the Pier;
Others, of Amusements tire,
They, real Rest, and Peace, desire.
Coming from the City's riot,
All They want is rest and quiet.
'Tis a ticklish task, and teasey,
Not so easy, not so easy;
'Tis I fear, an Order tall
E'en to Hope to please them all.
But we know they'll do their best
to please North, East, and South and West.

It also prompted the newspaper editor to conduct a ballot in August 1929 to asses the public mood. The results were clear: 2,658 Penarth residents voted in favour of the speaker while only 36 voted against; 200 visitors also voted in favour. This probably helped the Council make its mind up to purchase the speakers.

One hundred new deck chairs were also bought for the Esplanade at 6/- each to be available for hire at 2d for a morning, afternoon or evening period. A new approach of returnable deposits for bringing back the deck chairs was considered to be inappropriate for the type of visitors coming to the town. The Council clearly still believed visitors to Penarth to be somehow superior and more reputable than those frequenting such resorts as Barry.

The Penarth Chamber of Trade established a Publicity Committee for the town and approached the Council for financial help. They made several suggestions including a "Come to Penarth" campaign by advertising Penarth at railway stations as "Holiday at Penarth. The Garden by the Sea", the erection of direction boards in the town, converting the old pier pavilion into a skating rink or dance hall and the arrangement of flower shows, water carnivals and concert parties. No money was forthcoming, although the Council did concede that they might advertise the Pier and Baths. The Publicity Committee suggested that Penarth should emulate the success of Weston, but a member of the Council rebutted this comparison by remarking that they would never develop Penarth into a resort such as Weston. Music was suggested as a means of enthusing visitors to stay longer. The Council clearly saw the Publicity Committee as a bunch of mavericks and stuck to their usual programme. The big crowds on

PUBLIC NOTICE.

To the RATEPAYERS and RESIDENTS of Penarth.

The OBJECTS and POLICY of the PENARTH PUBLICITY ASSOCIATION for the FUTURE PROSPERITY OF THE TOWN are as follows:—

1.—To advertise Penarth as a HOLIDAY RESORT by means of PICTORIAL POSTERS on every RAILWAY STATION in Great Britain and in certain centres in Foreign Countries. The distribution of Illustrated Brochures, GUIDES and LISTS OF ACCOMMODATION throughout the Country. By means of Advertising Penarth in the Principal NEWSPAPERS.

2.—To delevop Penarth as a Seaside Resort, and induce VISITORS to spend their Holidays in the Garden by the Sea.

3.—To encourage people to come to PENARTH to live, and thus help to fill the large number of houses and shops that are now empty in the town. N.B.—There are Twenty-five Shops and 79 Houses empty at the time of going to Press, with approximate loss in rates of £2,000 per annum.

4.—They do not suggest the spending of one penny from the rates upon any scheme unless it would prove of a remunerative character.

5.—They have the full co-operation of the Great Western Railway Company, who have agreed to spend Pound for Pound in advertising in conjunction with this Association. Up to date over 2,000 Pictorial Posters of Penarth, together with 20,000 Illustrated Folders, have been distributed throughout the United Kingdom and New York, U.S.A. The Association has spent over £100 in Publicity.

6.—As a result of their Publicity Campaign, accommodation is now being arranged for 200 Visitors from Lancashire for a week during the coming season, in addition to the constant flow of enquiries the Secretary is dealing with.

7.—They were responsible for the organising of the National Orchestra of Wales Concert from Penarth which was broadcast by the B.B.C. They suggested the Loud-Speakers and the Deck Chairs on the Esplanade, which have proved a splendid investment for the town.

8.—The Association are desirous of filling the Empty Houses, Shops, and Boarding Establishments in the town, to reduce the rates, not increase them. They therefore take this opportunity of asking the Ratepayers of Penarth to support those Candidates who pledge themselves to support the aims and objects of the PENARTH PUBLICITY ASSOCIATION.

The PUBLICITY CAR BALLOT TICKETS will be on sale at Easter —Buy one and help our Funds.

H. SALTER, General Secretary.
THOS. CADDY, President.

An explanatory Public Notice from the Penarth Publicity Association in the Penarth Times in March 1930.

August Bank Holiday were entertained with loud speaker music and a concert, with a harpist and string quartet, in Alexandra Park. Two problems on the beach emerged that summer. There was a plague of flies and gnats which brought much discussion over spraying - they did not. Then there was glass on the beach which prompted the Council to put the first wire litter baskets on the Esplanade. To add to local excitement, that was the summer the sixteen year old Edith Pannell swam from Penarth to Weston-super-Mare.

Nevertheless, the Committee were not to be put off by the attitude of the Council. They swung into action and produced 2,000 posters for railway stations throughout England and Wales with the Great Western Railway meeting half the cost. Such advertising was much easier now, because the whole of the railway system in South Wales was run by the G.W.R. In 1922/23 the Penarth Harbour Dock and Railway, the Penarth Extension Railway and the Taff Vale Railway had grouped with many other small companies and amalgamated with the G.W.R., which became one of the four large companies that ran the railways until nationalisation in 1948

The Committee also organised the first Great Town Carnival, which started on Wednesday 18th September. Elaborate decorations were hung along the Esplanade, fairy lights and Japanese lanterns hung in the Italian Gardens and the Old Pier Pavilion was decorated and illuminated. They organised a 12 mile road walk, swimming races from the Yacht Club to the Pier, a Confetti Battle, side-shows on the Pier and dancing on top of the shelter and in the Old Pavilion. There was also a draw for a 1930 Morris Minor Saloon car.

The Carnival certainly attracted the crowds. Trains and buses brought thousands of people and Campbell's laid on a special steamer excursion from Weston-super-Mare. By 9 p.m. the whole area was jammed with an estimated 45 thousand people who were there to see the fireworks display. It was thought a great success by all, although some annoyance was caused by a bather who had 'the audacity to remove his costume on the beach'.

The Carnival was thought to be a great idea and the Committee developed it into an annual event, continuing to advertise Penarth in many well-known national newspapers. People came and the venture seemed to be a great success. In 1931, Jack Payne, the then famous BBC Dance Band leader, was even persuaded to come to open it. Mrs Payne came as well but she was so upset by the sight of penniless young children staring at the amusements that she gave some money for them to be entertained on the side shows.

However, there was a major disaster. On August Bank holiday that year, the wooden Pavilion at the end of the Pier caught fire during a dance. destroying the pavilion, the main length of the decking and the shelters. The Fire Brigade managed to stop the fire reaching the new Ballroom while boats from the local yacht club rescued people from the far end of the pier. Fortunately nobody was killed, although the structure of the pier was badly damaged.

The Penarth Pier Fire

THE BLAZING PIER

THE SCENE THE NEXT MORNING

(Penarth Times).

It was not reported if the fire was visible on the other side of the channel. If it was, then the people of Weston-super-Mare might have felt a little twinge of satisfaction because in January, the previous year, Penarth people watched with dismay Weston's own Grand Pier burning from Penarth Head, Cliff Walk and Rectory Road.

The Pier was repaired by the next season at a cost of £3,157 but, without the Pier Pavilion, the use of the new Pavilion for revues and variety shows was short lived. In April 1932 it reopened as a cinema, but even this was not a success and closed in June 1933. Then, in 1934, it was renamed the Marina and opened as a dance hall to take over the function of the old pavilion.

The pavilion reopened as the Marina.

Car parking without the yellow lines (post-marked 1930).

The restored pier after the fire with its new shelters. Deck chairs are stacked against the railings and an ice-cream man peddling his tricycle (post-marked 1942, but clearly a pre-war photograph).

All of these new developments were certainly changing the face of Penarth, but they were also killing off many of the old attractions. Before the first world war there were so many donkeys for hire on the Esplanade that the town was sometimes referred to as 'Donkey Island', but the last two donkeys licensed for hire were sold to a Barry man at the start of the 1929 season. There were only two rowing boats licensed for hire that season, although the Council were encouraging people to apply for licences to hire speed boats and saloon motor launches. The increase in private cars and buses was creating a need for a car park and there were complaints about the unnecessary use of motor cycles on the Esplanade. At the same time, the *Penarth Times* was reporting that the Cabmen's Shelter in Plymouth Road was little used and deteriorating.

Further suggestions for public works were put to the Council in October 1930 by a deputation of unemployed men. They suggested a bathing pool across the beach, the start of the Cogan Recreation scheme, the laying out of Cliff Fields as a pleasure ground, the construction of a public shelter at Cogan and a public convenience at Cliff Walk. Parliament, in 1931, rejected the proposed Channel Tunnel project which made more public money available and local authorities were encouraged to apply for grants.

In 1932 the Council spent £42.10s.6d. repairing the Yacht Club slipway and providing rental lockers on the pier for fishermen.

A couple of developments also went ahead in the town centre which produced much discussion. The first was the construction of a roundabout in Windsor Road in November 1936. This might not seem an important event to us now, but it certainly was then, because the only other roundabout in the area was near Llandaff in Cardiff. People actually went to watch the buses and lorries negotiating this new hazard in the town.

The second was the redevelopment of the Washington Hotel site. The owner of the Washington Hotel had given the Council first refusal on the site and there was talk of converting it into a new Town Hall. The Council had declined so it was sold to developers who decided to create what was described as a shopping and amusement centre. The plans were drawn up by Messrs Willmore Brothers ltd and made public in October 1936. The new cinema was described as being designed on the latest modern luxury designs to seat 1,300. The shops and self-contained flats above were to be set back about 15 feet from the existing boundary to allow for a much wider pavement. The *Penarth Times* descibed the redevelopment as 'a credit to local enterprise and a splendid example of town development that might well be emulated.' This development went ahead as planned except for the proposed lock-up garages.

The Washington Hotel and the Development Scheme.

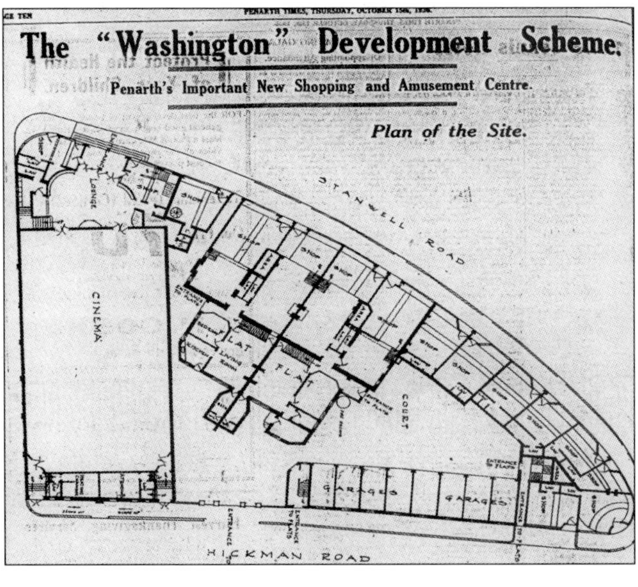

Apart from the loss of the Pier Pavilion, the continued success of Penarth as a sea side resort seemed assured even though the beach itself was even less attractive than it had been. Sand was noted to be being lost from the beach in 1930, then in 1932 black mud started to settle. The prime corner spot opposite the pier and next to Beach Villa was also seen to be a mess.

The deterioration of the beach continued and by 1937 the amount of mud was causing great concern and bathing was impossible at low tide. This was always blamed on the diversion of the river Taff through the building of the Alexandra Dock at Cardiff and the necessity to employ dredgers to keep the shipping channel open. Nevertheless, the crowds continued to come. In late August 1932 there was a heat wave which led to many people staying on the esplanade and beach until midnight. Many of the caterers took advantage of this and stayed open themselves. The local press reported that there were 500 people bathing on the beach on Sunday 18th August inspite of a lack of provisions. They were even having to change on the beach!

There was added excitement that summer when, on July 3rd, the Graf Zeppelin flew over Penarth at about 1500 feet on a coastal flight from Porthcawl to Newport before turning south for home. Perhaps the crew were just enjoying the view, or were they taking photographs?

Special events were continually being catered for. For example, over Easter weekend and Coronation week in 1937 the pier, esplanade, baths and beach shelter were strung with fairy lights and the Italian Gardens were floodlit. To close Coronation week, the Cardiff Post Office Band gave a Saturday evening concert on the Esplanade which was followed by a fireworks display from a floating pontoon, while rockets were fired from the pier. Fireworks, of course, continue today to be an attraction at Penarth's events.

The pier with the Coastguards station (Dated August 19, 1943).

Windsor Gardens

They continued to be a venue for many varied but selected events. For example, in July 1926 there was a rather grand affair when the Royal Society of St. George held a Rose Garden Party as its first function. The Lady Mayoress of Cardiff opened this event which had stalls, folk dancing, the Cardiff Post Office Band and a concert party. The proceedings from this garden party went to the Cardiff Royal Infirmary.

The Rose Garden Party (Penarth News).

However, even with the added attractions that were staged in the Gardens, the number of visitors steadily decreased. This was, no doubt, largely because of the close proximity of the free Alexandra Park and the Esplanade. It must be noted, however, that the Gardens must have been still popular for some because the *Penarth Times* carried adverse comments about the 'romancing' that was taking place there. Moves were eventually made by the Town Council to acquire Windsor Gardens. In the Autumn of 1928 the Earl of Plymouth eventually offered to sell both Windsor Gardens and the beach foreshore from a point opposite the Seven Sisters to near the Penarth Fort (roughly 180 acres) to the Council. Members went to St. Fagans in October to discuss the offer, which led to a flurry of criticism in the press about the apparent secrecy of the matter. Questions were asked about the use of the Gardens and the two Lodges, with the suggestion that one could be used by the PierMaster instead of spending £1,000 on building a new house. A draft agreement from the Plymouth Estate, in October 1929, offered to sell the foreshore to the Council, therefore saving ratepayers the £30 per annum ground rent of the Pier Pavilion and the foreshore land built over for the widening of the Esplanade. The Windsor Gardens and its lodges were offered free on the understanding that an old employee of the Estate,

Mr Carey, could live there rent and rate free. Although the arrangement seemed simple, the actual hand over of the Gardens took rather a long time. There was a hitch relating to the fencing which lead to further criticism over the long delay. Eventually, the whole agreement between the Council and the Plymouth Estate was made public in December 1930. In it the Estate would sell the foreshore for £1,700 and give the Council two pieces of land near the shelter at the top of Beach Road subject to a payment of £35 for improvements already made. Subject to the purchase, the Estate would give the Windsor Gardens, together with the two lodges, bandstand and other buildings. The Council had to allow the use of the South Lodge by Mr Carey, keep the trees and shrubs trimmed so that they did not obstruct the sea view of those houses fronting the garden, permit the continued use of the private gates, keep the yacht club slipway in repair for 108 yards and grant facilities for its use by the club.

This may have seemed straightforward, but clearly was not. There were several looming problems. The bridge over the dingle needed painting and both lodges needed a complete refurbishment. The Council agreed to installing a bath in the lodge to be used by the Piermaster, but not in the one to be retained by Mr Carey. The Council decided to close the Gardens almost for the first half of 1931, while the remedial work was being undertaken. A few other 'improvements' were made which did not meet with everyone's approval. The hedges were cropped to prevent any privacy in the seats - courting couples were not to be allowed in a Penarth public park unless they were in full view and acting in a proper manner. Railings were also placed along the edge of the path, ostensibly as a safety precaution against children falling off the cliff. The *Penarth Times* took the popular view that they were intrusive and ran several articles deploring the action of the Council, arguing that keep off the grass signs were preferable and considerably cheaper.

On Saturday 30th April 1932 the Earl came to the Gardens to open them to the public and at the same time declare the Windsor Road Dingle open. Thousands of residents came to watch, even though heavy rain fell during the ceremony. In his speech, the new Council Chairman, Mr George Moon, made much of the fact that Penarth now had 62 acres of parks and open spaces which was 3.5 acres per 1000 people and, therefore, 0.5 acre per 1000 people more than was provided for in the Town planning Scheme. He then thanked the Earl for this gift of 4.5 acres, to add to the 42 acres that his family had already given, and presented him with a gold key to the park. The manager of the Pier Pavilion Cinema took a film of the proceedings but its present whereabouts, if at all, are unknown.

The town now had a lovely park overlooking the sea that was stocked with a variety of shrubs and flowering trees that was described, rather optimistically, by the *Penarth Times* as second to none in the County of Glamorgan. The town's garden staff took over the responsibility for maintaining the Gardens and the Head Gardener's salary was increased by £12 *per annum* for his additional responsibilities. One drawback was that money was soon needed to be spent on a new water tank, on new railings that were generally thought to be unsightly and opening the park to the public also brought the inevitable problem of litter. But perhaps the most bizarre fact was that the Council provided no signs to indicate that it was now a public park, resulting in many summer visitors staying out, because they though that it was still private.

Unfortunately, it seemed that the council's attention was diverted away from Windsor Gardens, so that by 1937 much work urgently needed to be done. The bridge was unsafe and the council decided that it would be a waste of money to repair it and a replacement steel bridge too expensive at £499. It was subsequently removed leaving only the southern supports remaining to show us where it once stood. Shrubs and trees were also removed to give more space for fetes and to open up the views over the channel.

Alexandra Gardens

These gardens remained a popular place for the locals and visitors. Bands continued to come from many places to play in the park with early favourites being the concerts by the Cross Keys Silver Band and the Canton Salvation Army Band. Promenade concerts were also popular and included such local favourites as the Penarth Juvenile Choir, who sometimes took silver collections to support their activities. Nevertheless some local residents expressed the view that these concerts were wasted in the Park and that they should be staged on top of the Beach Shelter for the benefit of a larger number of people.

The park shelter soon became a popular place for locals to sit and on fine days a group of retired gentlemen, master ship owners and sailing ship masters met here to watch and talk about the ships. Other locals began to talk about them as the Penarth Parliament.

Efforts were continually made to improve the park with new shrubs and summer plantings. Then, after the end of the First World War an army tank was brought to the park as a presentation to Penarth in recognition of the large number of war bonds that were sold in the town. It stood above the bandstand until it was taken away in 1937 to supply old iron for the War Office Department. It was never popular and a much more appropriate flower bed now stands in its place. Because the flower beds have names, it is perhaps not surprising that this one is now called the tank bed. In contrast, local people did not approve the removal of the Alexandra Park and Windsor Gardens guns for the same purpose.

The ornamental fish pond and fountain were added to the parks attractions and this corner soon became a popular place for visitors. Nevertheless, signs of council economies later became evident because in 1927 there was a complaint in the *Penarth Times* that the fountain was only switched on for high days, holidays and the Wednesday afternoon half-day closing. Originally large goldfish were stocked in the inner part of the pond and dace in the outer, but the effects of continual thefts have gradually led to a reduction in fish content.

The traditional Prince of Wales Feathers flower bed below the shelter (post-marked 1920). Today replaced by a Scout badge.

The lower path in Alexandra Park.

In 1923 the Council decided to erect a War Memorial to Penarth's dead. Then came the debate on where to site it. There was a suggestion to purchase the triangular piece of land at the entrance to cliff walk and put it there. The majority of Council Members, however, preferred Alexandra Park, so that is where it was errected. The imposing marble War Memorial was designed by the famous Welsh sculptor Sir William Gascombe John and unveiled on Armistice Day, November 11th, 1924 by two Penarth women who had both lost three sons in the war. The *Penarth Times* reports that it poured with rain throughout the ceremony, but the area was packed and the nearby tank served as a grandstand for many of the onlookers. Immediately the proceedings ended the rain, of course, stopped.

The War memorial after its unveiling. Designed by Augustus John, it is a white granite stepped obelisk with a seaward-facing bronze winged victory standing on a ship's prow and holding a laurel wreathed sword. It was rededicated in 1958 by the Bishop of Llandaff and representatives of the Free Churches after the names of those who died in the second world war had been added. One track of the tank is visible to the right of the plinth.

Developments within the park continued. In May 1928, a rockery was constructed at the top entrance. A sundial made by the Head Gardener was placed on the terrace above the bandstand in April 1931. Sadly it was broken and removed a few years ago. Then, in December 1931, the Plymouth Estate offered several pieces of land to the Council including the path alongside Alexandra Park running from the lower Dingle bridge to Rectory Road. The Council found it to be in a deplorable state and decided to incorporate it into the Park. Many people objected to this because they were to lose a useful public footpath, but the Council took no notice and had the iron railings realigned to incorporate the path.

An increasing demand for bedding plants necessitated an additional greenhouse being built in 1937, alongside the existing one, near the park keeper's lodge.

The shelter and memorial viewed from the fishpond (post-marked 1926).

The Garden of Remembrance

This garden was first laid out in the 1920s, but it was never a very popular place for a great number of local residents. Many local people had become pacifists because of the large number of local men that were killed in the war. This, combined with the fact that there was a widespread 'Quaker' tradition in the town, led to an avoidance of anything that might be seen to glorify death in war. It was probably a recognition of this feeling that made the Council decide to authorise payment for the War Memorial instead of asking for donations. The Council took the same line when the names were added for the victims of the second world war.

The Garden of Remembrance was restored during the second world war and in the late 1940s the Remembrance Day Parades started to visit the Garden on the way to the War memorial.

The Garden of Remembrance.

Cliff Walk

Large numbers of people continued to use the Cliff Walk footpath so in 1913 four seats were put there. There must have been some conflict over using the path because in 1921 a notice was erected warning people not to cycle along the path. There were also many events on the nearby Cliff Field. For example, Penarth Rugby Club's week Fete in 1926 attracted about 8,000 people of which the majority were season ticket holders. Nevertheless, the Cliff Walk and Penarth Head that year cannot have been very pleasant places to be because many people were so badly bitten by mosquitoes that they had to seek treatment from a doctor. The *Penarth Times* in September advised people to dust flowers of sulphur into their stockings and garments to keep the insects away.

The Coastguard Signal Station was erected here during the first world war, although subsequently used for commercial shipping. It closed on March 1st 1929, but was not demolished until 1957 (post-marked 1924).

In November 1928, Councillor Deverall suggested that the Council should purchase the triangular piece of ground at the top of Cliff Hill Road at the entrance to Cliff Walk for the purpose of laying out a miniature golf course or putting green. The Plymouth Estate was approached about its purchase and it offered to sell it for £860.10s.0d. which the Council thought reasonable. Discussions then went on for several months in the Council and through the local press. Although a few people thought the amount asked was too much, most people believed the idea to be a good one especially as it would prevent other developments taking place at the very entrance to Cliff Walk.

Eventually, in May 1930, the Plymouth Estate wrote to ask the Council if they had made up their mind, but clearly they had not because they promptly started looking for other possible sites for a putting green. In response to an enquiry, the Plymouth Estate offered a plot of land (5,200 square yards) between the Dingle and Bridgeman Road for £1,300, but the town surveyor thought its size unsuitable for a putting green so this land was finally built on. The land at the top of Cliff Hill Road was eventually included in the agreement covering the foreshore and Windsor Gardens and was effectively purchased for £35. Meanwhile private enterprise overtook the Council's efforts. A putting course was opened in 1931 on Cliff Walk Field and proved to be very popular. There was some local concern, however, that building might still occur on the site.

Soon there were sales of ice-cream at the entrance to Cliff Walk and of light refreshments from the now redundant look out station.

The cliff walk beyond the gate at the Seven Sisters was gradually deteriorating and dangerous. Cliff falls were numerous and sometimes took sections of the path with it. The *Penarth Times* sent one of its reporters for a walk along the path who didn't seem to be enthusiastic about his experience. The surface was found to be very rough and pot-holed and there were sudden and dangerous drops to the beach below. The reporter even thought that he might not have returned if it had been raining and the ground became slippery. In view of the unstable nature of the cliffs it is surprising to find that there had been a suggestion of steps up the cliffs between cliff walk and the Seven Sisters and a, hardly appropriate, comparison made with beach access at Ilfracombe.

Penarth Head

The Council were always keen to develop this areas but plans were continually frustrated by the Government's defence plans. The headland was partly restored as an open space after the Great War when agreement was reached between the Council and the Military. The sum of £674.9s.6d. was approved for the cost of restoration and four seats were put there for people to enjoy the view. A small rockery was built in 1922 and a shelter installed in 1926 being one of a pair bought from Bouton and Paul of Norwich that year. A drinking fountain was completed in May 1928. Pressure was put on the Council to spend money on restoring the right of way on the land requisitioned by the Government. The Council was clearly not prepared to do this as they wished the right of way restored to the pre-war condition before they took it over again.

The open space has clearly always attracted a lot of people. Unfortunately in 1940 the Council heard that certain 'undisclosed offences' were alleged to have taken place there and quickly decided that the open space should be closed at night.

Principal Parks, Recreation Grounds and Open Spaces
owned by the Council in 1938 *

Alexandra Park	(Pleasure Park)	6.5 acres
Windsor Gardens	(Pleasure Park)	4 acres
Esplanade Gardens	(Pleasure Park)	1/4 acre
Athletic Field	(Recreation Ground and Tennis Court)	13 acres
Cogan Playing Field	(Recreation Ground)	16 acres
Llandough	(Recreation Ground)	2 acres
Plassey Square	(Children's Play Ground)	2 acres
Belle Vue Gardens	(Bowling Green and Putting Course)	2 acres
Cliff Walk	(Open Space)	11 acres
Penarth Head	(Open Space)	1 acre
Windsor Road Dingle	(Open Space)	4 acres

* An advertisement appeared in 1938 for the appointment of a working Head Gardener and Parks Superintendent at £180 per annum rising by annual increments of £10 to £220 per annum.

THE SECOND WORLD WAR YEARS 1939-1945

In the late 1930s the town was still clearly competing with Tenby to be South Wales' premier seaside resort, rather than with the nearby Barry Island and Porthcawl that were attracting an ever increasing number of day trippers. This approach clearly had its effects on visitor attraction because the *Penarth Times* commented that Midlanders often had never heard of Penarth although they knew of Barry and Porthcawl. There was even a proposal, by Mr Mills of Cowper Close, that was debated at the Council meeting in January 1937, to change the name of the town to Penarth-on Sea in order to attract more visitors. This idea was rejected because of the unemployment situation in the town. The dock was idle and 40% of the men living in Penarth were out of work. A change in name was thought detrimental to the Council's request to the Ministry of Labour to have the town classed as a special area. The war of course changed all this as men enlisted and others were called up. The docks reopened for war service in July 1940. Cargoes of ammunition, bombs, planes, vehicles, locomotives and petrol were sent from here all over the world, but especially to the North Africa campaign. The docks were used by the Royal Engineers for training as stevadores and also by the US Navy. The Americans arrived early in 1944 and left in July that year for the Mediterranean zone. Fortunately the docks were undamaged during the war and, alongside the more obvious war efforts, supplied the west country with coal.

The idle docks. The building in front of the coal-shutes was the 'Flying Angel' Penarth Mission to sea men. These Missions were established to provide something for the sea men to do instead of drinking and womanising. Mr W. Bently was the last Port Missionary when the Penarth Mission closed in November 1936 (post-marked 1927).

Penarth Council continued to develop its tourism strategy and promoted the town up to and during the Second World War. The Parks Committee decided, in February 1940, not to advertise Penarth for holidays although the Parks and Open Spaces would continue to be made attractive. It appears that there was a general interest throughout the whole country in preserving parks for the public. In May 1941 the South Western branch of the Institution of Parks Administrators held their first ever spring meeting in Penarth. After a short talk by the Chairman of the Council they visited Alexandra Park, Windsor Gardens, the Athletic Field and the allotments at Mountjoy Road and Fairfield Road. The weather was ideal and the members were enthusiastic about what they saw.

Praise also continued to come quite often from many visitors. For example, in 1940, Mr Flemming of Roundhill, Bolton, who had written on the subject of parks, recalled a statement by Mr Clough Williams-Ellis, a champion of rural preservation, which said Penarth to be unique in being the only town where there is a conspicuous absence of ugly advertising hoardings obliterating the natural charm of its surroundings. All this confirmed the belief of the local residents that they were living in what was described as 'The most beautiful little town in South Wales.'

The war, of course, brought some changes to the town. Air raid shelters were erected around the town, in Cogan Playing Fields and the Athletic Field, while Barrage Balloons were anchored at Cogan Playing Fields and Plassey Square to protect the Docks. The town sustained some air raid damage, especially in the Paget Road area, and on one occasion in June 1941 the Alexandra Park greenhouses were broken. There was discussion about turning the parks over to allotments for the duration of the war, but the Council initially chose to requisition Plymouth Estate land on Stanwell Road. Later they agreed to using half an acre of the Cogan Recreation Ground, the Windsor Road Dingle, Belle Vue Garden and Mountjoy Open Space for allotments. Two plots on the south side of Windsor Gardens and three flower beds in Alexandra Gardens were also set aside for vegetable growing. Some use must also have been made of the greenhouses in Alexandra Park because the Superintendent sold tomatoes to the public on at least one occasion. Luckily the parks did not suffer too badly when the Ministry of Works and Buildings requisitioned iron railings and gates in the Spring of 1942. The surveyor could exempt railings on artistic or historic merit or if they were necessary for security, so those in Alexandra Park and Windsor Gardens survived, although those enclosing the Italian Gardens were removed. There were even some improvements to the parks themselves. For example, in February 1940 in Alexandra Park the uncultivated dingle in the hollow near the glass houses was opened up for public access. A dry-stone Pennant Sandstone wall was built to retain the bank, steps constructed down from the upper end and a section of crazy paving laid at the park entrance end. Then in 1942 a new flight of steps was constructed in Alexandra Park around the old sea water tanks from near the lower entrance to the Bandstand area.

The war did not stop visitors from continuing to come in large numbers, causing the *Penarth Times* to comment on the need for an air raid siren on the very popular front. The number of organised events also seemed to increase rather than decrease. In War Week in June 1941 there was a general parade from Stanwell Road to the Recreation Ground where the Earl of Plymouth took the salute. There was amateur boxing in the Marina Pavilion and the Cardiff Co-optimists appeared nightly, at 7.30, in the Windsor Gardens with their gala night on the 12th June attracting 700 people. The week was obviously a great success bringing in £15,000, which was three times the planned amount.

The Esplanade and the Beach remained open the entire time, although access to the beach was prohibited between sunset and one hour after sunrise. The Pier remained open as well for promenading and fishing, although the War did, however, bring about a severe reduction in the numbers of White Funnel steamers coming.

When Penarth entered into the spirit of the 'Holidays at Home' campaign in 1942 the numbers of visitors increased again. Transport to and from the town became a real problem with Bank Holiday trains and buses unable to cope with the crowds that came. The town itself just about managed, with all the available deck chairs usually taken early in the day. Many people sat and listened to the gramophone concerts played over the speakers from the Beach Shelter. Bands often played on the Promenade to add to the attractions of the town and the Windsor Gardens were used for dancing in support of the St John's Ambulance Brigade. In the summer of 1943 the visiting crowds became so large that bookings were stopped in Cardiff by the Railway Company because the Ministry of Transport regulations prevented them putting on extra trains. On one Sunday evening in June a couple of hundred people, most of them hot and tired women and children, were left at Penarth railway station because the trains were already full of people returning from St Mary's Well Bay. As the bus area was also overcrowded many were forced to walk back to Cardiff. One note of austerity appeared in 1943 when bathers had to supply their own towels in the swimming baths.

The limited transport did not put people off visiting Penarth and in 1944 the crowds were back and on a blazing hot Easter Monday the parks, Esplanade and Baths were overflowing. Then on Whitsun Monday many records of visitor numbers were broken: 1,600 chairs at 3d each were let on the Esplanade, 4,000 visited the pier, 900 swam in the Baths and 250 cycles were left in the cycle store under the Public Shelter. Later that year, on Sunday September 7th, the street lights were switched on for the first time in five years and crowds of singing youths congregated on the Promenade.

The view along Plymouth Road, from the junction of Holmsdale Place, towards the station.

PLYMOUTH ROAD

Out of Penarth's Plymouth Road,
That chaste align of red brick,
Cardiff's mysterious docksmen flit,
Blonde secretaries and discrete clerks,
Subalterns chasing for a game of darts,
Dry educationalists of Morgan's vale,
Seadogs blustery as Norwest gale,
Linen drapers, mild and pale,
Bankers carrying chips or fruit,
Black market shoppers slim and cute,
Dark Spanish beauties, or ordinary cuties,
Indigenous pearls, commonplace,
Walzing Matildas, valentines,
Woofs, kittens, cats and porcupines,
Armed with the current "Penarth Times,"
Rush with the channel's sure and pet,
And frown on sturdy Somerset.

Penarth Times, 20th September 1945.

THE POST WAR PERIOD

The end of the war in Europe (VE Day: May 10th 1945) was celebrated by hundreds of people thronging the sea front and the flood lit Italian Gardens. Bonfires were lit around the town, with the biggest on the dock beach, and there were many street parties. The Marina Thanksgiving Ball was open for dancing until 1am with tickets costing 10/6 each, including refreshments. The attraction was so great that there were too many people on the floor to dance, but nobody seemed to mind. Victory over Japan (VJ Day: August 16th 1945) brought more celebrations and bonfires. Nearly 3,000 people crowded the Esplanade to dance in the road and the Italian Gardens to music that ranged from waltzes to jitterbugs.

After the war, the Council continued in its efforts to attract visitors to the town. New planting were made in the parks and chain link fencing erected at the front of the Italian Gardens in 1947 by A.J.Binns, for £98.8s.9d., although not before 'wanton and malicious damage was done at the weekend by youths'. Penarth Head Open Space was also fenced for £75 and notice boards erected in prominent places in the parks to show closing times. It was also agreed to continue the controversial war time arrangement of opening of the parks on Sundays. New licences were issued for pleasure boats to operate from the beach, fishing competitions started on the pier, and Punch and Judy shows on the beach (though not on Sundays) and gramophone record programmes initiated. A 'collecting mine' was put on the Esplanade for the Shipwreck Mariners Society. At one time these mines were to be seen at every seaside resort in the country, but many have now gone

People came once again to the beach to swim and August Bank Holiday 1946 brought in huge numbers of holiday makers producing long queues at the beach side cafés. Many others brought hampers and boiled kettles of water on fires of collected sticks or of coal that they had carried with them. Although the weather was fine there was little else to do except swim or try to listen to the music coming from what many described as 'loud squeekers.' Complaints about the quality of the speakers eventually led the Council to decide, in September 1949, to discontinue broadcasting. Mr Douglas Baid of 'Uppercliffe' immediately conducted his own poll arguing that 429 out of 431 people wished the service to continue. The Council relented and started the programmes again.

Car parking became an increasing problem with vehicles often filling both sides of the Esplanade, Cliff Road and most of Bridgeman Road. In 1945 the Government had announced aid for local authorities to build underground car parks, but this idea did not appeal to Penarth Council. Instead they turned to the Cliff Field area. They paid £750 for land and banned parking on Cliff Road. Unfortunately they did not signpost the new car park, so most visitors remained unaware of its existence. The increasing parking restrictions lead to many letters being sent to the local press. One visitor wrote to the *Penarth Times* 'Penarth is a most uncivil sea side resort where the motorist is hounded from pillar to post' adding that he could not recommend anyone with a car to visit the town. That was mild, compared to 'Disgusted' who wrote in 1949 suggesting that a very large White Board should be erected at the top of Cogan with big red lettering 'We do not want visitors in Penarth. Please bear right for Barry.'

"Sitting in the sunshine on the Esplanade" in April 1947 (Penarth Times). Judging by the clothes it must have been a cold day to sit in the sunshine.

There were a couple of set-backs to the Council's plan to revitalise Penarth as a premier sea side town. In May 1947 the Canadian steamer Port Royal Park was driven by a gale broadside into the pier damaging much of the pier's structure. A Bailey Bridge was considered as a temporary measure but was too expensive an option at £3,000. Another scheme for ferrying passengers to the steamers was turned down by Campbell's as not viable.

Tugs trying to pull the Port Royal Park away from the pier (Penarth Times).

The Piermaster inspecting the damage (Penarth Times).

Rebuilding was done by George Carter (Erection) Ltd costing about £28,000 and the pier was not reopened until Whit Saturday, 1949. The old shelter at the seaward end was not replaced. The official opening was on the 4th June by the Chairman of the Council, Mr Gareth Roberts JP. A small party boarded the Glen Usk to meet the Captain and then rejoined the main party for refreshments in the Marina Sun Lounge. Campbell's paddle steamers started their regular visits again and their two new ships, the Bristol Queen and the Cardiff Queen, were soon regarded as the finest paddle steamers anywhere in Britain.

The pier during its reconstruction before the shelters were replaced. A crane is still in position half way along the pier. This view from the italian Gardens must have been photographed in the summer of 1948 because the chain-link fencing has been erected.

The timing of the reopening was good because in March that year the Government lifted its ban on ornamental lighting. So by the end of May there were fairy lights on the pier and floodlighting in the Italian Gardens. In May two speed boats were operated from the landing stage by Mr Boyle who had paid £75 for the concession. Speed Developments Ltd paid £25 a year for the sole rights to operate a photographic service on the Esplanade and pier. Light refreshments were sold on the Esplanade from a trolley and there was a Punch and Judy show once again on the beach. A lifeguard was also employed for the summer.

Things were looking up, but a major problem at the time was oil pollution and spoilation of many of the South Wales beaches. Tankers still cleaned out their tanks at sea and lumps of sticky black oil washed up on the beaches. I can clearly remember stopping swimming at Jackson's Bay on Barry Island for the same reason. In 1951 officials went from Penarth to a conference of Glamorgan coastal authorities to discuss the problem. Unfortunately, it was a problem that remained for many years. The sighting of a small school of porpoises quite close to the pier in September 1949 was not to be repeated. The worst case of pollution occurred in mid February 1972 when a 250 yard long oil slick was washed onto the beach.

In April 1949 the Council purchased the Paget Rooms, which had been operating as the Regal Cinema for many years. They spent nearly £4,500 adapting it for its present day function as a multi purpose hall.

Accidents continued to occur on Beach Hill, with a 13 year old girl being taken to Cardiff Royal Infirmary with concussion in April 1944. It is interesting to note the Council's reaction to these accidents. After many years of deliberations and a rejection of any suggestion of altering the curve of the road, it was decided in 1949 to erect signs and stencil the road with an order for cyclists to dismount. The accident rate dropped although many people ignored the signs.

Two brighter spots during this period were the Festival of Britain and the Coronation of Queen Elizabeth II when the town tried to regain some of its pre-war festive spirit. The Coronation celebrations were much more organised and included band concerts on the Esplanade and at Cogan Recreation Ground, a torchlight procession and many street parties. There were more street parties on June 1st 1969 to mark the investiture of the Prince of Wales.

A typical advertisement of the time (Penarth Times).

In 1953 the Institute of Parks visited Penarth while at their annual meeting in Cardiff. Meanwhile, the economy was showing some signs of picking up and people were increasingly using cars. The result was that the police fixed No Parking signs on the Esplanade later in the year.

However, holiday patterns were changing and passenger demand for the paddle steamers was declining. In 1959 Campbell's ships started to be withdrawn from service and scrapped and the remainder of the White Funnel Fleet moved from Bristol to Penarth during the winter of 1958/59. The company made one rather bold experiment in the summer of 1963 when a hovercraft (SRN2 - 001) was hired for an experimental six weeks service from Penarth to Weston. Bad weather and a damaged skirt rather curtailed the service, so it was not repeated again. By 1966 the Company was loosing too much money and decided on rather drastic action. The Cardiff Queen was withdrawn from service berthed in Penarth Dock until 1968 when she was broken up.

In 1964 Penarth Council decided to extend the annual weekend Regatta into a holiday week. It was considered a success and continued as an annual event. New events were tried out in successive years such as the Channel Water-ski Race in 1967, when the winner went from Penarth to Weston-super-Mare and back in 76 minutes, and the first Round the Houses Cycle Race in 1969.

An advertisement for the 1968 Holiday Festival (Penarth Times).

Three photographs of the 1965 Holiday Festival (Penarth Times).

Windsor Kinema

Telephone 72.

To-day, Friday and Saturday.

ROY ROGERS and —————
————— GEORGE (GABBY) HAYES

— in —

MY PAL TRIGGER

(U). A dramatic story featuring Trigger, the smartest horse in the movies.
At 3-30 — 6-5 — 8-40.

— ALSO —

GLENN VERNON and MARCY McQUIRE

— in —

MELODY MAKER

(U). A romantic comedy with music. Hollywood the setting, and a sensational boy pianist to entrance you with his playing. At 2-15 — 4-50 — 7-25.
Doors open Thur., Fri., 4-25. Saturday 2 p.m.

Monday, 9th, June, for 3 days.

EVELYN KEYES and KEENAN WYNN
WITH ENRIC MADRIGUERA AND HIS ORCHESTRA

— in —

THE THRILL OF BRAZIL

(U). Come on a joy and laughter ride in glorious Rio.
At 3-0 — 5-45 — 8-30.

— ALSO —

JAMES HARCOURT and PATRIC OWEN
WITH THE ARTEMUS BOYS

— in —

THE GRAND ESCAPADE

(U). The story of three boys who have an exciting time roaming the countryside with a wandering junkman's caravan. At 1-45 — 4-30 — 7-[illegible]
Doors open Mon., Tues., 4 p.m. Wed. [illegible]-30 p.m.

Thursday, 12th June:

PENITENTIARY.

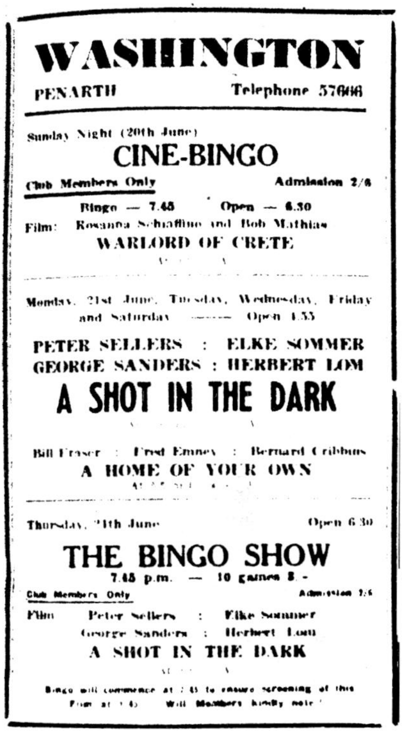

WASHINGTON

PENARTH Telephone 57608

Sunday Night (20th June)

CINE-BINGO

Club Members Only Admission 2/6

Bingo — 7.45 Open — 6.30

Film: Rosanna Schiaffino and Bob Mathias

WARLORD OF CRETE

Monday, 21st June, Tuesday, Wednesday, Friday and Saturday ——— Open 4.55

PETER SELLERS : ELKE SOMMER
GEORGE SANDERS : HERBERT LOM

A SHOT IN THE DARK

Bill Fraser : Fred Emney : Bernard Cribbins

A HOME OF YOUR OWN

Thursday, 24th June Open 6.30

THE BINGO SHOW

7.45 p.m. — 10 games 3/-

Club Members Only Admission 1/6

Film Peter Sellers : Elke Sommer
George Sanders : Herbert Lom

A SHOT IN THE DARK

Bingo will commence at 7.45 to ensure screening of this Film at [illegible]. Will Members kindly note!

Changing cinema choices. The Windsor Kinema (1947) and the Washington, advertising films and bingo (1965) (Penarth Times).

The town crests of St. Pol de Leon and Penarth who twinned in 1968 (Penarth Times).

There were other near misses for the pier. In 1968, on a foggy day in August, the Bristol Queen approached the pier too fast and hit it. Luckily the damage was not great, repairs were minimal and sailings were not interrupted. Unfortunately, the following summer the Bristol Queen smashed her port paddle while cruising off Barry and was taken out of service. Although there was talk of preserving her, the ship was towed to Holland the following year for breaking up. Cruising then only continued from Penarth Pier and other places in the Channel on the motor ships St Trillo, Westward Ho and Balmoral. In 1980 the paddle-steamer Waverley, now owned by the Paddle Steamer Preservation Society, sailed south from the Clyde for a short summer season in the Bristol Channel. From then on she and her sister ship, the motor vessel Balmoral, have been regularly calling at Penarth Pier.

An advertisment in the Penarth Times for Celebration Cruises in the Bristol Channel in 1997. The Waverley - The Last Sea-Going Paddle Steamer in the World - was built for the London and North-Eastern Railway in 1947 but has been owned by a Registered Charity for 23 years. The Waverley and the Balmoral regularly cruise from Penarth Pier during the summer months.

The New Westminster City off Penarth Head. It was refloated on the second attempt (Penarth Times).

In October 1969 an oil tanker went aground 200 yards off the pier but tugs managed to refloat it. Then in 1987 the 11,376 ton cargo ship New Westminster City ran aground off Penarth Head while being manouvered through the deep-water channel to Cardiff Docks. Perhaps the original objection to having a longer pier was a good one.

Cruising in the Bristol Channel.
The Bristol Queen (above) in 1965 and The Waverley (below) in 1989 (B.A.Thomas).

The increasing use of cars was one reason for the demise of the paddle steamers and the cars themselves brought problems to compact towns like Penarth. There were simply not enough parking places.

Traffic conjestion during the 1965 Holiday Festival (Penarth Times).

After many years of discussion the Council decided in 1968 to spend £100,000 or more on constructing a multi-storey car park on the beach. They abandoned the other idea of building across the railway line between Stanwell Road and Victoria bridges. There were many complaints, especially from the residents of Sea Bank, but the Council went ahead. When it was finished it was described as 'A gleaming white reinforced concrete structure with pleasant longitudinal lines harmonizing with the landscape and merging into the cliff at the rear.' Fears that it would be a monstrosity were said to have disappeared. I beg to differ.

Other plans for the car park met with as much, if not more, opposition. The ground floor was planned to have some other use. Penarth Leisure Centre Ltd (Mr E.Rabaiotti and Mr D.Berni) wished to develop it with games that were mainly for children. Residents of Sea Bank were especially vociferous in claiming that it would lower the concept of Penarth as a 'Garden by the Sea', bring discredit to the area and bring it to the level of Barry Island. The Glamorgan County Council rejected the application, although subsequently the development of the ground floor did go ahead. Another proposal was to add a fourth floor for use as a helicopter landing pad. It was never followed up, so we have no idea how the locals or the County Council would have reacted to that.

Water-ski and power boat clubs used the slipway under the multi-storey car park, but in 1969 the Water Ski Club made a proposal to have a club house on top of the Esplanade shelter.

An artist's impression of the original design for a water-ski club house on top of the Esplanade Shelter. A later design was for a more elaborate brick built structure. Fortunately neither was given planning permission (Penarth Times).

Luckily this proposal did not find favour. Instead, it brought a wish to have the roof restored as an access between the Windsor Gardens and the Esplanade. These new steps, costing £4,000, were a project of Penarth Civic Society for European Architectural Heritage Year. Half the money came from the Wales Committee for European Architectural Heritage Year, £500 from the Vale Council and the rest from donation and efforts of local people through such organisations as the Round Table and the Ladies Circle. They were opened in June 1977 with the Lord Lieutenant for Glamorgan, Sir Cennydd Traherne, leading the official party up the steps. So today it is once again possible to climb directly from the roof of the shelter to Windsor Gardens. The Esplanade shelter itself is still in need of repair although the toilets facilities were improved in June 1995 at a cost of £95,000.

The Pier Pavilion was reopened in September 1970 as the Commodore Club and Restaurant and continued as a dance hall for several years until it was refurbished in the late 1980s as a snooker club. Major structural work to the pier over the last few years has necessitated the closure of both the pavilion and the pier. The whole restoration scheme is likely to cost over a million pounds, but should ensure that it survives into the foreseeable future.

The Baths were an ever increasing problem for the Council. The small pool was closed in 1966 following an outbreak of the rare disease swimming pool granuloma that summer. Then followed several years of discussions on constructing new baths within a recreation centre. The Drill Hall in Woodlands Place was the first option but there was not enough space. The Kymin then became the favourite option for a £250,000 recreation centre with sports hall, squash courts and a swimming pool that could be linked to the nearby multistorey car park. The situation became even more confused when an American considered building a 200 bedroomed hotel in the Kymin with its own swimming pool, but this came to nothing. Finally in 1971 the decision was taken to abandon the idea of a recreation centre and to spend about £2,500 refurbishing the old baths. This was done but, in November that year, another problem arose when Penarth's beach was reported to be one of the dirtiest in the country. Some local people immediately wanted the baths converted to fresh water. Penarth's Medical Officer of Health tried to allay fears about the beach by stating that bathing in sewage polluted water carried only a negligible risk to health. The Council were assured that the treatment for the baths sea water was good enough so they voted 7 to 2 in favour of retaining sea water. Despite these many years of indecisiveness by the Baths Board, the Baths remained open until 1985. After closure they were sold for private development and reopened in 1991 as the Inn at the Deep End. Also in 1991 the Baths' sea water tanks that remained in Alexandra Park, were filled in and trees planted on the site.

In Windsor Gardens the northern lodge was sold and is now a private house, while the southern lodge is an art gallery.

There was a move in 1976 to close the children's paddling pool because of the need to clean it once or twice a day. The cost for new pumping and cleaning equipment was thought to be too great. In contrast a paddling pool on the Esplanade could be kept adequately clean. However, when Welsh Water's pumping station was built at the entrance to the car park the Esplanade pool was moved closer to the sea wall. It may yet become a flower bed, although the decision has been delayed. Meanwhile the car park is itself the subject of a planning proposal to create private apartments, offices, shops and a restaurant in a five-storied 'ocean liner' design building.

Local Government reorganisation came on the 1st April 1974, so the years of discussing whether or not to join with Cardiff came to a head in 1972. The recommendation to the Government was that Penarth should be with Cardiff as zone 1 in the new South Glamorgan. Penarth Council did not want this and made a good case for joining with Barry and Cowbridge as zone 2. This was accepted as an amendment to the Local Government Bill in the House of Commons Standing Committee, so Penarth became incorporated into the newly established Vale of Glamorgan Borough Council. The new body took control of all the amenities in the town including the parks, playing fields, esplanade, pier and swimming baths. The Town Council now only has responsibility for the Kymin,

St Augustine's Triangle and the Pembroke Terrace Amenity and Play Area. The creation of the new Unitary Authorities on April 1st 1996 did not alter this arrangement although the Town Council would have liked to have gained control of the parks and playing fields again. However, although the Vale Council is the local planning authority it has a statutory duty to consult the Town Council on all planning applications relating to the town.

Suddenly in 1987, emergency action had to be taken by South Glamorgan County Council because the Esplanade pavement started to collapse. The reinforced concrete top of the 1930s Esplanade extension was cracking. For a while the area was simply roped off while everyone waited for the Vale of Glamorgan to do something. The estimate of £250,000 was considered prohibitive so the Council appeared to do little else than pour concrete into the void. But in 1988 it was the Cardiff Bay Development Corporation who stepped in and paid for the repair and complete refurbishment of the front. The ballustrade was replaced, the walkway raised and paved with red bricks and buff slabs, the seats were renovated and 30 additional lighting columns were fitted for a total cost of £100,000. Cardiff Bay Development Corporation also upgraded the Paget Road Play Area.

In October 1991, Her Royal Highness The Princess of Wales visited Penarth and unveiled a plaque in the Italian Gardens to mark the refurbishment of the Esplanade. Flowers were laid here following her tragic death on August 31st this year.

The first flowers laid in the Italian Gardens following the tragic death of the Princess of Wales. The message read: 'To Diana. We love you because you loved children like us. Love from Robin and Sarah.' (Penarth Times).

The Centenary Celebrations were held for the Pier in September 1994. The Esplanade was closed for the Sunday celebrations on the Esplanade and Pier and many people wore Victorian costumes for the occasion.

The 'best' Victorian costumes of Mrs Liz Smith, Jessica, Mathew and Isabelle on the Esplanade (Penarth Times).

Cutting the special 100th anniverary cake on the pier (Penarth Times).

A new lifeboat station was constructed in 1996 at the base of Cliff Road to replace the inshore life boat station situated in the old deck chair store under the Promenade shelter. Planning was approved in June 1994 after waiting several months for details of the proposed slipway. An appeal was launched to raise £100,000 towards a new lifeboat - a 24 ft Atlantic 75 capable of 34 knots and being used in the dark. The first sod for the new station was cut by the Lord Lieutenant for South Glamorgan, Captain Norman Lloyd-Evans, on February 2nd 1995 and the completed building opened in June 1996 by Her Royal Highness Princess Alexandra. She also named the new Atlantic 75 inshore lifeboat the 'Spirit of Penarth'. The construction of the new lifeboat slipway prompted the Vale Council to recommend removing the old concrete beam slipway opposite the Yacht Club; the slipway that came to Penarth in the agreement with the Windsor Estate in 1930.

Princess Alexandra opening the new Lifeboat Station (Penarth Times).

Destruction

The 1960s was a boom building period which unfortunately resulted in many fine buildings being taken down to be replaced by blocks of flats or small groups of town houses. This is most noticeable on the sea front where Rock Villa and Balcony villa were demolished in 1963 and the Windsor Court flats built on the site in 1965. This redevelopment had been made more feasible when the lessee of the corner plot relinquished his interest in order for the Council to improve its appearance. The impact on the building line was tremendous although the more recent tile cladding and pitched roof line has done much to improve the old concrete block image of the original structure. The Seabank flats were built at the bottom of Beach Hill in 1965. The Esplanade Hotel closed in 1971 and was allowed to deteriorate and rot away. It was bought in 1976 by a local businessman who made several unsuccessful planning applications for blocks of flats in its rear garden. These applications were all turned down because of the impact that the flats would have had on the view from Alexandra Park. But on a Sunday in late May 1977 the whole situation changed. Fire badly damaged the domed roof and gutted the top two floors of the Hotel and it was never rebuilt. It was subsequently demolished in the late 1980s with Alexandra Court being built in its place and houses in the rear garden.

The view back from the Waverley in 1988. The original uncompromising lines of Windsor Court dwarf Speed's Esplanade Buildings while Seabank dominates the view to the north of the pier. The multistorey car park is just visible behind and through the pier. The spire of Christchurch is still on the skyline (B.A.Thomas).

Elsewhere in the town there have been changes with many old mansions being converted into flats or being demolished for new developments. The Cory's house, Seaview, in Bradfield place had become a school but was demolished in 1963 and replaced by five blocks of flats, collectively known as Seaview Court. The 1860s Hollies, on Beach Hill, has been replaced by Albany Court. Cliffside, which was built in 1919 at the end of Forrest Road for Sir Sven Hanson, has also gone to be replaced by a small estate of modern houses. The

1880s Roxburgh, in Plymouth Road has also been demolished. It had been bought from S.A.Brain (who moved to Cwrt-y-rala House) in 1909 by Tom Morel, the ship owner and chairman of Morel Ltd and his widow Constance lived there until her death in 1968. With only a few years to run on the lease, it was handed back to the Plymouth estate. It was sold, the house was demolished and the present landscaped town house development built in the grounds. The grand Northcliffe, on Penarth Head, has gone. Originally built in the 1840s and called Cliff Villa, it was home to several important residents including John Batchelor. It was demolished in 1969 and Northcliffe flats and Mariner's Heights built in its grounds. This development could have been a complete visual disaster if the original plan for an eleven storey block had been passed. Fortunately, both Penarth and Glamorgan County Council rejected it as completely unacceptable. The Penarth Dock Master's house, built in 1864 and called The Ferns, has been recently replaced by a small development of houses of the same name. Undercliffe Drive has been built on the site of the coastal gun battery. In 1969 houses were built on a private garden of 1.33 acres which was the last open piece of ground on Marine Parade. The Council and Glamorgan County Council once again both rejected a much grander and visually intrusive scheme. In 1967 there was talk of demolishing the Washington Cinema and some of the adjacent shops but this did not happen.

The railway closures, prompted by Lord Beeching in the mid 1960s, led to the withdrawal of passenger services from Penarth to Cadoxton on May 6th 1968. The line was closed between the Penarth Cement Works and Biglis Junction and the track lifted. The Council at the time considered buying the station bridge and the sidewalk for pedestrian access. It is a pity they did not. When the Cement Works closed in 1969, the line beyond Penarth Town was closed and the track lifted, The track from Penarth to Cogan Junction was reduced to a single track operating from the old up platform side. The original limestone-built town station was for many years used as commercial premises. However, one weekend in 1990 it was demolished to be replaced by the present redbrick block of shops clearly designed to complement the elaborate Station Hotel next door which itself has been rather aptly described as 'elephantine cottage orné.

Even the churches have not been safe from the developers. In 1988 Plassey Street Presbyterian Church was demolished. It had been empty for a number of years before being used as the Tent House but then the Penarth Jehovah's Witnesses wanted to build a new Assembly Hall there so it had to go. Christchurch United Reform Church in Stanwell Road was then demolished in 1989. Bethania Chapel in Hickman Road has also gone, while St Josephs in Harbour View Road has been converted into flats.

Some changes are still taking place. The 1901 Holme Towers in Bridgeman Road, designed by Edwin Jones of Cardiff, has been replaced by the hospice of the same name. Despite much local protest, two more houses in the same road have also been demolished, but at least they have been replaced by red brick buildings with some style and not 1960s concrete blocks. Thankfully the gothic-styled Ty-Llwyd still survives.

At least there are no intrusive tall blocks in the town centre. There are only Seabank on the front and the six storey building in Plymouth Road which was built in 1964 as a Methodist Church sponsored hostel, International House, for 50 students from all over the world. It is now part of the Waverly Home.

Princess Margaret meeting Francis Akinselve, from Nigeria, while opening International House in 1965 (Penarth Times).

The Docks were finally closed in 1963 and partly filled in with rubbish. The subway that had been under the River Ely in 1900 was closed and blocked up in 1963. In October 1970 the Docks were sold for £500,000 to a local man, Mr Norman Harvey. After various schemes of development were talked about and tries out, the seaward end of the Dock was restored as part of the Portway Marina and Portway Marina Village development. Over 75,000 cubic metres of silt and mud had to be dredged and new lock gates fitted before the first boats could enter on Saturday June 20th 1987. The Secretary of State for Wales, Mr Peter Walker, opened the Portway Village Village on September 25th 1987. Cardiff Bay Development Corporation have sealed the rubbish tip and announced that they will be creating a new park here.

The view across the outer Marina towards the lock-gates. The tall crane is working on the Bay Barrage (B.A.Thomas).

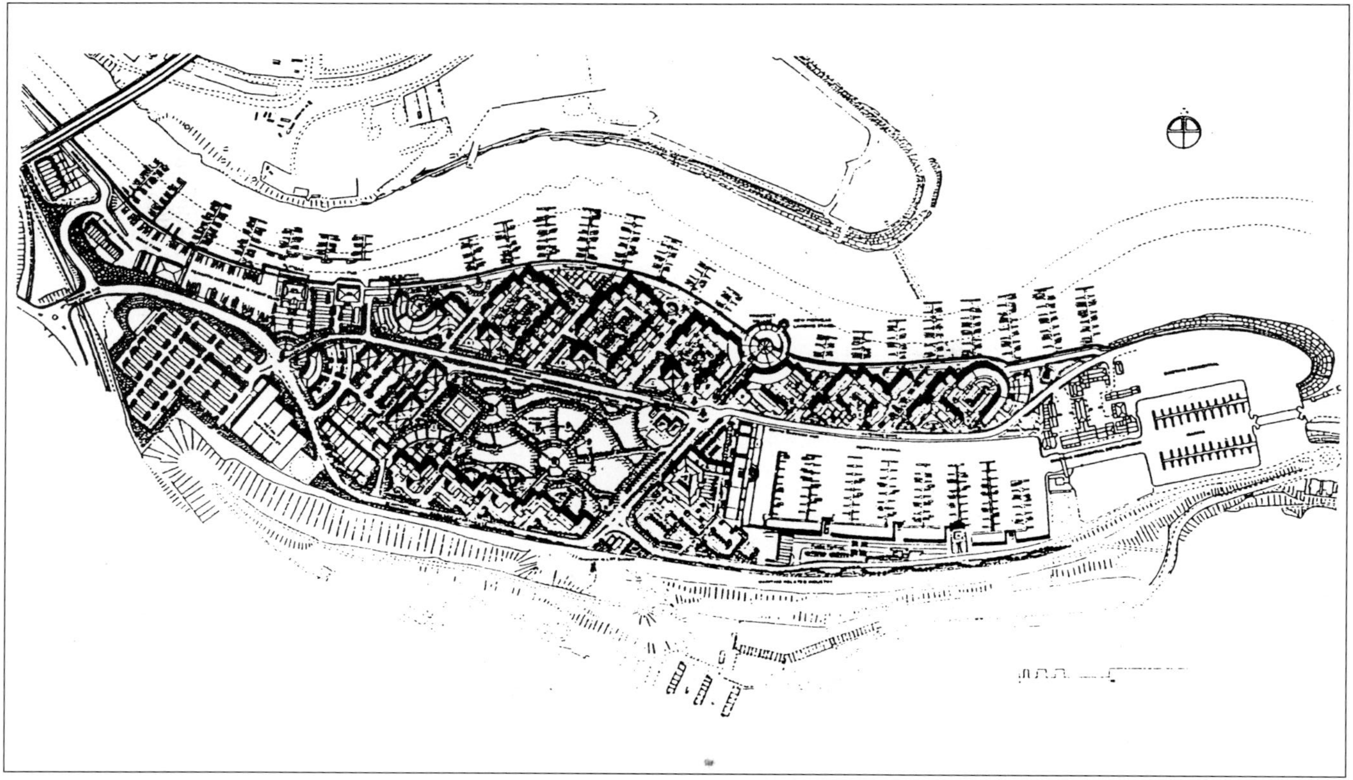

The original Penarth Haven Masterplan produced by AMEC Regeneration showing the proposed 550 homes, up to 90,000 sq ft of offices, three to six acres of light industry, the central park, riverside walks, shopping and leisure facilities (Penarth Times, May 1991).

Looking across the inner Marina towards Cardiff (B.A.Thomas).

Survival

The parks and gardens are thankfully still relatively intact. The Italian Garden is still an attractive place in which to sit and watch the world go by. Very little change has been made to the original structural layout except that the original iron railings were taken away during the second world war. Two fine Yews flank the central steps and Agaves and Palms give the feeling of a southern seaside resort. A splendid fig tree also adorns the south facing wall of the shelter, but.unfortunately very little else remains of the original scheme of planting. The new pillars and wave-design railings along the esplanade were installed in 1994 and instantly attracted mixed feelings. Over 2,000 people signed a petition asking for them to be removed, but to no avail. The disabled access walkway was added in 1995. Greater ease of access to the Italian Gardens and shelter has been made possible by the narrowed zebra crossings.

Windsor Gardens remain relatively intact although the urinals were closed in the late 1950s because of their substandard condition. A recent development in the Gardens has been the planting of the Holme Tower daffodil walk called the Field of Hope. The plaque was unveiled on Saint David's Day 1993 by the Town Mayor, Mr Nigel Gibbs.

In Alexandra Garden, the Bridgeman Road entrance was improved by filling in a depression on the Esplanade Hotel side and grassing it. Concerts were then effectively brought to an end when the bandstand was removed. An estimated cost of £62 for repairing damage to it was considered too expensive in 1951! A shelter from Belle Vue Gardens was brought there to stand in its place and now contains the aviary. Thefts of budgeries in 1987 necessitated new stronger grills that were added in January 1988. The seats provided for the visitors to the concerts are still there for people to sit in the sunshine even though they now surround the aviary.

Unfortunately, other changes have removed many of original features. The weather station that was installed in 1956 was removed in the early 1980s and a young cedar now stands rather incongruously in its place inside the railings. Then in 1994 the shelter was removed and replaced by a 'Victorian style' bandstand at a cost of £20,000 and the Lodge was sold off as a private house. In the same year the Vale Leisure Committee approved in principle the idea of spending £70,000 to replace the greenhouses with an Alice in Wonderland-style maze. Unfortunately it was given a low priority and is unlikely to be built in the near future. Children had lost out for a second time, because in 1968 a plan to spend £2,250 on building a paddling pool in Belle Vue was shelved in response to the Government's appeal to cut back on public spending.

The topiary birds in Alexandra Park (postmarked 1947).

The Dingle, from Plymouth Road to Bridgeman road, is still a pleasant wooded valley with many of the original oaks still standing and the magnificent tree at the Bridgeman Road entrance to Alexandra Gardens must surely be the oldest one in Penarth. Unfortunately the Dingle is now somewhat in need of care as overgrowth, sycamore invasion and rubbish are spoiling its attraction. What appear to have been ponds have silted up and are now overgrown

The view southwards along Cliff Walk. The chimney in the distance is at the South Wales Portland Cement and Lime Company's works at Lower Penarth (written and dated 1942).

The field adjacent to Cliff Walk was finally purchased in 1952 and named Cliff Green. It was not officially opened until 1956 and a nine hole pitch and put golf course provided the next year. A slight problem arose over golf balls constantly landing in some nearby front gardens, but it was overcome by repositioning some of the tees and holes.

In 1957 the old coastguard look out hut was demolished and plans made for a new development to include a shelter, a children's play area, toilets, an attendant's office and a lock up shop. Since that time the area has been generally improved. The play area is fenced off and a more safe surface provided. There is a new coastguard station and an enlarged restaurant and shop, now Cioni's, which was built in 1987.

Cliff falls continue to be a problem at both ends of the beach. The *Penarth Times* reveals ongoing criticism of the state of the path to Lavernock, since the 1920s, especially again during the early 1940s and up to the present time. It was clearly deteriorating and thought to be highly dangerous in places. Indeed there had been several instances of near fatalities. One of the worst was in September 1945 when eighteen year old Clifford James fell and injured himself badly. He had to crawl along the beach to the Yacht Club slipway before he could attract someone's attention to his plight. A few months earlier a woman had fallen but suffered only minor injuries. These incidents caused great concern so in August 1946 a fresh path was cut further away from the edge. The town Council eventually asked their surveyor to advise the Glamorgan County Council on the best action to take to slow down the rate of cliff fall. For this, the surveyor argued that he needed to consult records dating back to 1838. In 1976 the Vale Council contracted a £3,000 report on how to protect the coastline and footpath. The engineer suggested two actions: a borehole drainage system at a cost of £15-20,000 and a protective wall at the bottom of the cliff together with trimming of the upper part followed by grassing at a cost of £15-25,000. The Council were taken aback at the cost and decided to make do with trimming the face. However discussion continued and eventually a length of protective wall was build at the base of the cliff.

At Penarth Head nearly all of the searchlight and battery remains have been washed away and since the 1940s a strip of land about 30 feet wide has been lost taking with it a tarmac path, steps and expanses of lawn. Worry over children climbing the cliff-side fence prompted the Council in the early 1950s to use barbed-wire as a deterrent. Recent suggestions to reduce the falls have included sealing the cliff in polyurethane foam, sealing the top with a membrane as in Penarth Haven landfill site and making a concrete walkway along the base. In May 1988 the *Penarth Times* explained that the extension of the Esplanade, as a Second Phase Barrage, would involve the demolition of the multi-story car park and the construction of a new promenade with leisure use, landscaping, car parking, walkways and beach access to a new harbour village. The private sector would probably finance the development which was not scheduled until some time after 1994. It now seems rather unlikely that such a development will ever take place and, even if it did, I for one would not feel too confident about strolling along immediately underneath such an unstable cliff.

TOWN PARKS AND OPEN SPACES

The increasing population of the expanding town needed parks and open play areas of its own, The sea front gardens and open spaces were all very well for a gentle stroll, but the locals wanted places where they could relax or play games. There were of course patches of undeveloped land where the children played, but there was nowhere for organised or competitive games. As early as 1889 a petition of ratepayers asked the Local Board to provide a recreation ground, but they were merely told to see Lord Windsor about the matter. Nothing happened for several years so a further deputation made a similar request in 1893. The newly formed Council established a Committee in June 1895 for the purpose of reporting on ground for recreation. They approached Lord Windsor who offered to help. So once again the town found itself the beneficiary of further gifts of land from the Windsors and proceeded to develop a few parks and open spaces throughout the town.

The number of parks and open spaces gradually increased over the years that followed. As the town spread, the type of housing changed with open spaces planned into the developments. For many years the Council feared misuse of the public land so they were usually fenced and subject to strict byelaws. It was not until 1951 that the Council relaxed Sunday use and permitted children, up to school leaving age, to play games in all Council owned recreation grounds. Even then organised games were still prohibited. In the early 1950s open air childrens' evangelical church services were being held at Wordsworth Avenue playing field and St Cyres Park and occasional Sunday Schools at Plassey Square. Public attitudes have changed in recent years, many of the railings have been removed and there is a much more relaxed attitude to the use of the playing fields and recreation grounds.

The following account of the other parks and open spaces in the town is relevant to the development of the town as a sea side resort. Without these parks and open spaces, there would have been more pressure put on the older parks which might not have survived in their nearly original forms. The details I have given are not meant to be an exhaustive treatment of their history, but to supply an overview of their development to fulfil the town's recreational needs.

Arcot Street Shrubbery

This small piece of land opposite the Royal Hotel had been given to the town by the Windsor Estate in 1889, but was left for many years as undeveloped open space. A shelter was erected in 1889 to replace an unsanitary urinal. However, by 1903 there were many complaints about nuisance because of the shelter. Notices were placed in the shelter reminding users of the byelaws, but this seems to have had little effect. The locals seemed to treat it as their own piece of land, so further shrubs were planted in the early 1920s partly to prevent the unauthorised grazing of horses. However, the area was constantly vandalised and even the public shelter was partly destroyed and taken away for firewood. For many years the area was then used as a car park, but recently was restored as a County Project undertaken by school children, although in this case with a little adult help. It received a Prince of Wales Award when Prince Charles visited the town in 1982.

The restored Arcott Street Shrubbery today. (B.A.Thomas).

Plassey Square Recreation Ground

This gently sloping piece of land was also given to the town by the Plymouth Estate in 1889. At first it was a piece of rough open land to the rear of Plassey Street, but in 1900 the streets laid out around it were called Plassey Square and the lane approaching it Recreation Avenue. Much later the top road was renamed Harbour view. The land was levelled in 1901 by the contractor Thomas Rees and has been left as an open area since then. It is, perhaps, interesting to note the attention that the Council took to running these comparatively small open areas. They put up an attendant's hut in 1927 and next year provided first aid equipment for it. Nevertheless, no water tap nor toilets were ever provided, even though the Council debated the issue several times in the late 1920s. It was then thought a good idea to have a sand pit here, but the Council decided against it on the grounds that it would become verminous. Later it must have become more difficult to maintain standards, because by 1943 even the hut was reported in the *Penarth Times* as 'going and soon to be gone'.

In 1926 Sunday opening of the Recreation Ground was agreed on a trial basis. However, there was so much ëhorseplay and bad language' while football was being played that the police were called in. This led to the *Penarth News* asking the question 'Will the Penarth Sabbath become as riotous as that of Barry?' When, in May 1927, the Council were debating opening up the pleasure grounds on Sundays the trouble at Plassey Square was remembered, leading to the decision to keep them shut.

Because of its relatively central position, the land has been used for many events over the years including fêtes and a circus, but it has always been left open for general use. The children's play area was first laid out in the late 1940s although it has been revamped since then.

The view across Plassey Square towards Taff's Well and the Rhondda Valleys (B.A.Thomas).

Cogan Recreation Ground

The open land at Cogan had always been a problem for the town because it was so low lying, easily flooded in winter and the permanent Cogan Brick ponds often smelled badly. In May 1887 there was a special meeting of the Council to consider the suggestion that sewage was being driven back into the ponds by the tide. Nothing effective appears to have been done because in 1903 the stench was reported to be so bad that the Council asked the Bute Estate owners to assist in filling in some of the ponds. Permission was given and they were filled with refuse. There were increasing arguments in the Council about Cogan being the poor relation of Penarth so, by April 1909, the Council had opened discussion with the Windsor Estate about the provision of recreational facilities on the open land. This resulted in fourteen acres of land being given to the town by Lord Windsor. The Cogan Playing Ground was officially opened on April 16th, 1911.

Cogan Playing Field Officially Opened

TWENTY-FIVE-YEAR-OLD DREAM COME TRUE.

PLEASING ENDING TO COUN. D. J. WILLIAMS' YEAR OF OFFICE.

"I NOW OFFICIALLY declare the Cogan Playing Field open to the residents of Penarth, which includes the residents of Cogan and Llandough, for ever."

WITH THESE WORDS Mr. D. J. Williams, J.P., Chairman of the Penarth Urban District Council, unlocked the gates with a gold key, presented to him by Mr. Edgar I. Evans, A.M.I.C.E., Engineer and Surveycr to the Council, for the official opening of the ground on Saturday afternoon.

(Penarth Times)

The cost of fencing and laying out 2 acres of the Cowslip field for games was £400. Unfortunately, although the area gave 11 acres for playing fields, the land was too hilly and clearly not very suitable for the purpose for which it was intended. By 1926 there was much discussion on the feasibility of exchanging it for the lower Old Brick Pit fields. Even this area was not perfect, because there were still ponds in which the locals reportedly threw dead dogs and drowned their unwanted cats. Heavy rain also brought problems and local flooding. In November 1926 the *Penarth Times* reported Bridge Street 'lake' overflowing its banks and referred to the area as the 'Land of Lakes'. The problem here was this part of Penarth was owned by Lord Bute and not Lord Windsor. An interview was therefore arranged between Council and the representatives of Lord Bute's Mountjoy Estates to see if the Estate would give the land to the town. Lord Bute never regarded Penarth in the same paternalistic way as Lord Windor so the Estate would not give the land but offered to sell at a price that the Council thought excessive. They turned down the offer in November 1927. The matter did not rest there, because a few years later the local press once again mentioned the need for a Recreation Ground and suggested the Brickyard field as the best option. Discussions resumed in the Council and, in November 1929, the Ministry of Health, the Carnegie Trust and the Playing Field Association were all asked for contributions towards the cost of buying the field and turning it into playing fields. Events continued to move slowly. In October 1930 the Council recognised that the discussions were muddled and confused and decided to proceed with the Government Unemployment Grants Committee scheme which gave 75% of the cost, but also to ask the Bute Estate to donate the land. Then came the question of compensating the tenant of the land, with the Estate suggesting that it was the Council's responsibility, while the Council was asking for vacant possession. Eventually it was all agreed and in 1931 the Council settled the problem with grant of £120 from the Carnegie Trust and the National Playing Fields Association. The new areas were laid out and opened in April 1932. There were now 11 good acres available for playing purposes, although the town surveyor had argued that it was necessary to retain the pond to act as a reservoir because the land was at the same level as high water on a spring tide. The pond was later filled with clean water to a depth of two feet for model yacht racing and for use as a skating rink when frozen in winter.

Mechanisation came to Penarth Parks in 1932 with a demonstration at Cogan of a mowing machine that would replace the four men who would need to be employed to continue to cut the grass by hand.

In 1935 the Council were again discussing the insanitary conditions at Cogan and the rat infestations of the pond, but nothing was done. It was not until 1947 that the pond was finally filled in.

There have been several attempt to create a new layout at Cogan. In 1947 the Council laid out a children's play area and planned to sell half an acre in exchange for the allotments. This did not proceed. In 1972 Penarth Council tried for the second time to incorporate a one acre former allotment area into the Recreation Ground but there was dispute over the ownership of some of it and they refused to agree to the demands for £750 in settlement. Then, in 1976 after the creation of the Vale of Glamorgan Council, the Vale Leisure Services recommended its incorporation. Meanwhile a proposal to erect a sewage pumping station at the Ground met considerable local opposition, with over 800 local residents signing a petition. The Town Council also objected and recommended its siting nearer the Docks and the Vale Planning Committee agreed.

The Government's Job Creation Scheme in 1976 gave the Vale Council the opportunity to develop additional pitches. These pitches were welcome, but it was the Leisure Centre that was to revolutionise sport and leisure in the area. The centre was opened in April 1985, twenty years after Penarth Council first discussed the idea of having one in the town.

The present day view across Cogan Fields towards the Leisure Centre (B.A.Thomas).

Belle Vue Gardens

The name came from Belle Vue Cottage which originally stood with its orchard and market garden where the now Council Offices were built in 1881. This move was prompted by the creation of the Town Council from the Local Board that year and by the need for it to vacate its space in the Windsor Estate Office at no.3 Windsor Terrace. The Town Council saw the triangular field opposite their new offices as a prime site for a public bowling green and other facilities for the people of Penarth and agreed in July 1908 to approach the Plymouth Estate about it. In December 1912 the Earl of Plymouth agreed to give the land to the town providing the Council paid £418 for the recent improvements and bore the cost of fencing and planting shrubs. The Council agreed and by November 1913 had decided to give its present name of Belle Vue Gardens. The Gardens were opened in September 1914 after a delay of several months caused by the contractor Lewis Brothers. The Parks Committee had discussed the possibility of erecting tennis courts on the site, but agreed that it was impractical to do so. Instead, the sloping land was developed as an open park and a bowling green laid out on the site of an old limestone quarry. The green was opened in 1922 and many members of the new Bowling Club were originally members of a club that used to play on a green laid out by W.H.Hancock & Co. in 1907 to the rear of the Penarth Hotel (later The Headlands School). The bowling green was enclosed in dwarf railings and a toilet erected.

Nevertheless, the Bowling Club was not an immediate success, even though reasonably priced season tickets were available, because there were many continuing problems over the condition of the green. For example, in May 1926 the green was officially opened, but immediately closed because of morning rain. In contrast, both Penarth Green and Windsor Green remained opened. In June that year the green was again criticised as the worst in the area and preparation for the coming seasons play unduly delayed. The Council had been debating how to improve the facilities for some time, because in April that year the Parks Committee had decided to issue season tickets for 15/-. However, comments in the *Penarth Times* made this out to be too dear and pointed out as well that only 20 season tickets were usually sold. This gloom was in marked contrast to the enthusiasm which greeted the opening of a new brick-built spacious pavilion and clubhouse at the Windsor Green when one hundred and sixty members and friends attended the special opening tea on May 29th 1926.

There was some trouble at Belle Vue with vandalism. In 1921 severe damage to the park by children prompted the Parks Committee to take the rather drastic action of writing to all the Headmasters and Headmistresses in Penarth to warn all children to "conduct themselves in a quiet and proper manner when in the gardens and cease destroying the shrubs etc." Putting courses were clearly a mania of the early 1930s and the serious possibility of having one at Belle Vue was costed at £55. It was also suggested that the shelter from Arcot Street should be moved here instead of moving it to Plassey Street so that there would be less chance of it being vandalised. The children's play area was built in the late 1940s and refurbished in recent years.

The new Town Hall, viewed across the field that was to become Belle View Gardens. The photograph is of Citizen's Sunday in 1908 before the start of the procession to St Augustine's (Penarth Times).

Belle Vue Bowling Green. The houses of Albert Crescent lead to St Augustine's Church.

Windsor Road Dingle

The Council were given this wooded valley by the Plymouth Estate in 1920 with the intention of providing some tennis courts. There was, however, little sign of activity for many years until in early December 1926 there was talk in the Council about filling it in with rubbish. Discussions were subsequently entered into with the Great Western Railway, whose surveyors suggested that there was a need for a sewer, a culvert and an unscaleable wall between the Dingle and their railway. By the end of the year an agreement appeared possible and in early spring 1927 tipping began with demonstrations of new motorised refuse collection both here and at the 'Billy Banks' tip overlooking the dock. Objections soon started to appear in the local press centried on the very slow rate of tipping, on the fact that the Council had already spent about £1,500 of ratepayers money and how the public were now prevented from using the area. By June 1928 the progress on tipping had speeded up and in December agreement was reached with the G.W.R. to remove a hillock dividing the Dingle from the railway for more space. Even so there was still much criticism in the press especially over spoiling the Dingle's natural beauty and the danger to the health of the local inhabitants. Meanwhile various suggestions were being made for the development after the cessation of tipping. A new shelter and seat were planned by the Council then there was a suggestion for a new road with an outlet through to West Terrace. Events, however, moved slowly and tipping carried on with the criticisms being now centred on the destruction of the trees.

Eventually, in April 1930, the Council announced that part of the Dingle would be opened as a children's playground, but then almost as an afterthought announced three weeks later that they had agreed to shoot the rooks in the Dingle colony because of a complaint from an allotment holder. Understandably, complaints poured in and the Council quickly reversed their decision and the rooks remained.

Thought was given to levelling the Dingle in 1930 and in April 1932 the Council discussed the possibility of siting a bowling green here or at Cogan Playing Field. The surveyor estimated the cost to be £300 but pointed out that the Dingle would not be available for some time. Then in May the Council approved a plan for exchanging land which would enable them to fill up the Dingle to a height of over 33 feet. This was done and apart from a threat of closing the Dingle just after the War the land has remained open and undeveloped since then.

Athletic Field

The Council accepted a gift of land from the Plymouth Estates, in 1920, for an Athletic Field. It was levelled for cricket and football and formally opened in 1924 by the Dowager Countess of Plymouth.

The Topical Talk column in the *Penarth Times* in January 1926 pointed out that the Council considered some time ago a proposal to increase facilities by addition of an adjacent playing ground. The question was asked as to why had the Council not done it, considering it now had the power to obtain additional open spaces for recreational purposes. This was perhaps a little unfair, because the Council's Parks Committee had already asked the Surveyor for plans for a new refreshment pavilion. However, they thought that the cost of £350 for a 30ft building with a 14 ft veranda and tea gardens was too expensive and asked for a cheaper plan. New tennis courts were also being laid out that year, although the work seems to have been rather slow. In July the Penarth Times again returned to the topic of extra land, pointing out that although the area was fully enjoyed by young people there was not enough available land in the winter when the Football Club closed off its area. This led to the radical suggestion by Councillor Humphries that the grounds be opened from 2 - 9 p.m.

The matter did not rest there because a few years later the local press once again mentioned the need for a Recreation Ground and suggested the Brickyard field at Cogan as the best option.

In June 1927 the Council opened the Field on Sundays and almost immediately received complaints about children riding bicycles and scooters and running back and for with prams. People thought that such unseemly behaviour on Sundays should be stopped. This problem was insignificant in comparison to that of Plassey Square so the Council, for once, seemed relatively relaxed about the complaints and did not interfere.

The present Athletic Club building was opened in 1972

Lavernock Road (St.Mark's) Playing Fields

Here is a mixture of open space and playing fields that were opened because of the increasing need for more sports fields. It was in 1926 that the Council first took steps to rent the field in Lavernock Road opposite Victoria Road for use by athletic clubs. By 1947 it was clearly time to extend the range of facilities for athletics clubs and the Council considered acquiring even more land there. The reclaimed land on the rubbish tip in the old Cwrt-y-Vil Quarry was first rented and then purchased in 1952 under the provisions of the Physical Training and Recreation Act (1937). The Welsh Department of the Ministry of Education granted £650 towards the total cost of £963 for purchasing, fencing, levelling and seeding the land.

Old Penarthians Rugby Footbal Club, which was formed in the early 1950's, now have their clubhouse here.

Golden Gates

In April 1926 the Bute Estate offered the Council a strip of land between Cornerswell Road and Coleridge Avenue. At the time it was being used as allotments, although most of the tenants had already quit. The Council accepted and, in deciding to initiate no immediate development, gave the remaining allotment holders five months to harvest their crops. At first, the use of the space as a park was objected to by most of the locals. To meet some of these objections it was proposed to put up gates at the two entrances and engage a local resident to lock the park at night at a cost of about £135 a year. The town surveyor also made it clear that it was planned to make it a park and pleasure ground. There would be a some seats and a few shrubs, but most of the space would be for children to play in. He did not want it to become either "an ornamental garden or a bear garden". The residents would still have access via their back garden gates. There was some hilarity in a Council meeting at the time when there was joking about walking on the grass being allowed, because there was only mud.

Misinformation was clearly rife at the time, because correspondence in both the *Penarth Times* and the *Penarth News* caused the Chamber of Trade to object to the supposed proposal to spend £135 each on two gates. Members of the Penarth Board of Trade thought the scheme to be a ridiculous waste of money in such an out of the way place. Their comments were mild compared to those in a

A 'Golden Gate' (B.A.Thomas).

meeting of the Penarth Anti Rate Payers Associated. They included many sarcastic comments about the money to be spent and suggested that the gates might be better made of nickel plate and marble or even better silver with the town arms inlaid in emeralds. They thought an insurance cost of £50 might be necessary as well. By mid April the *Penarth News* was referring to the 'Golden Gates of the Garden City' and reassuring its readers by the next week that they really were not made of gold, nor studded with diamonds, nor ornamented with pearls. The *Penarth Times* immediately followed by calling them the 'Golden Gates in Cornerswell Gardens. From then on both newspapers continued to refer to the Golden Gates and the name stuck for the gates and for the garden itself.

The children's play area in the Golden Gates park (B.A.Thomas).

An air raid shelter was erected there in the war, but has long since been taken down. In 1976 the Council returned to the original plan of using the area for young children. Following a series of complaints by the local residents, the Council restricted games to the under 12 year olds and banned ball games arguing that Victoria Fields and the Athletic Ground were not far away. The playing field today is still largely open and grassed with a small children's play area.

Redlands Road Recreation Area

There were tennis courts and grass courts here in 1926, and in April that year the owners of the Regent applied to the Council for permission to erect a stall for selling ice-cream and sweets. This lead to the Council asking the Surveyor to make enquiries about buying a suitable building from the Wembley Show for erection on the site for the purpose of letting to the highest bidder. By September there was clearly a great deal of mixed feelings about the idea for a letter in the Penarth Times urged the Council to drop it suggesting that at best the shops would be 3rd or 5th rate general stores and a general eye-sore. Now it is an open grassed field with a children's play area.

Redlands Road Recreation Field (B.A.Thomas).

Victoria Playing Field

This rough grassland alongside Coleridge Avenue, owned by the Education Authority, had formerly been allotments and the playing field for Victoria School. Children had always played in the field in the evenings and at weekends so in the early 1950s the Council asked the Education Authority to open the ground to children. Once again there were complaints by residents. Nevertheless, the Council accepted the need to retain the accessibility of the field and in 1955 reached an agreement for it to be open on Sundays. There is now a children's play area at the Coleridge Avenue entrance.

Victoria Playing Fields (B.A.Thomas).

Cornerswell Gardens Open Spaces

In the 1920s the Marquis of Bute's Mountjoy Estate was developing the Cornerswell Gardens housing on Paxton's Field at the edge of Penarth. Cornerswell Gardens had been designed along the lines of a garden city with a number of small open grassed areas. However, the Mountjoy Estate did not have the same driving force behind it as the Windsor Estate so progress was slow. For many years the roads were bad and the grassed areas little more than strips of mud. The Town Council steadfastly refused to take over the maintenance of the roads until they were finished.

Old and new children's play areas at St Cyres (Penarth Times & B.A.Thomas).

In November 1926 two open spaces were offered to the Penarth Mutual Housing Society (the residents of Cornerswell Gardens) which debated the issue and suggested they were given to the town. The Marquis of Bute promised to consider the idea and in February 1927 offered the two pieces of land to the Town Council with two stipulations. One should be laid out as a Persian Market enclosed by triumphal arches for children and the other 1/4 acre nearby should be laid out for the benefit of the public, possibly with tennis courts. The Council

At. Augustine's Church with the Open Space to the left (postmarked 1904).

debated the offer, talked about a bowling green and asked their surveyor for a report on the feasibility and the cost. The estimated cost was £1179 and £678 to improve and lay them out. The larger area facing Mountjoy Avenue was thought to be not big enough for a bowling green. The potential cost stalled any immediate action by the Council, especially in view of the unfinished nature of many of the roads. There was open talk of the open spaces being a burden rather than a gift. By 1929 conditions had improved in Cornerswell Gardens and the street works were virtually complete so the Council once again considered acquiring the plots. The Council members were still very uncertain but in 1930 they finally asked the Estate to donate the land, no doubt spurred on by talk in the press about the locals using them as rubbish dumps. The land was given, but there was to be no Persian Market.

The untidy state of the triangle of land at the junction of Mountjoy Avenue and Redlands road prompted the Council in May 1955 to enquire if the owners would give the land to the town. The land was subsequently designated as open space and the trees thinned. As usual there were almost immediately complaints about ball games being played there. The Mountjoy Crescent Open Space fencing was removed in 1956 to be utilised in other open spaces for replacing deteriorating fencing.

St Cyres Park

When housing was being planned for the St Cyres part of Penarth, the Council reserved a strip of open land dissected by a wood and stream for a park. The plan for the land was debated at a special meeting of the Council in August 1952 and the subsequent layout that followed remains virtually intact today. Two and a half acres are maintained as woodland and the stream culverted until it enters the wood. Unfortunately, the woodland is poor and the stream appears to be polluted. A footpath from St David's Crescent to Cedar Way dissects the land on the Morristown side with 2 acres being allotments and the land on the other side left undeveloped and overgrown. The open area on the St Cyres side of the wood has been maintained as a long informal open space with a children's playground. However, following a campaign by local parents and the Safe Children Penarth team, the Council in 1994 agreed to remove the old slide and roundabout and install new equipment on a safety surface where it is more clearly visible. It was enclosed in June 1996 by a bow top fence and animal grid at a cost of £8,000.

Other Open Spaces

There are a number of small open spaces in the older part of the town that are worthy of some mention.

The St Augustine's Church Open Space is a triangular piece of land that is still maintained by the new Town Council. It is probable that it was given to the town in April 1926 by the Windsor Estate. The nearby Pembroke Terrace Amenity and Play Area is owned by the Council.

There are two small triangular pieces of land in the Queens Road area. The Plymouth Estate gave the vacant piece of land at the junction of Queens Road and Lord Street in 1927, but the original ownership of the other is unclear.

The Council were offered in January 1971 the two acres of ground surrounding All Saints Church in Victoria Square. They leapt at the opportunity of having open space in this part of the town and accepted. The fence and hedge surrounding the area were removed and grassed over. Seats were then installed making it a pleasant parkland amenity for the town.

In December 1976 the Department of Leisure of the Vale Council approved a £2,000 scheme for an adventure playground on open space at Harbour View.

The Kymin

As early as July 1947 the Council decided to purchase the house and ground under a Compusory Purchase Order. There was constant talk of this for a couple of years with the owner countering by offering possession with a sitting tenant. Eventually it was agreed and it became the property of the town. Part of the Council's logic in acquiring the site was to create a car park for up to 500 cars. Presumably the idea was to take up virtually the whole lower part of this valley site. However, the multi-storey car park was constructed instead. Then followed several years of indecision over whether to build a recreation centre in the grounds, a subject which I have dealt with elsewhere. The grounds were used as a nursery for the parks and gardens, while the house was let as flats for a number of years. However, in the early 1970s the house was left vacant and it fell into disrepair. When the ownership passed to the Vale of Glamorgan in 1974 there was even talk of demolishing the house altogether. Fortunately it was renovated instead at a cost of about £50,000. The grounds were also tidied up and extra car parking spaces have been recently added.

Penarth Town Council had always wanted to retain ownership of the Kymin, but there was a legal bar on the Vale Council giving or selling the site. Instead it has been licensed to the Town Council for community purposes. The house is now used for community events and some classes. The Penarth Petangue Club also regularly meets in the grounds.

Cosmeston Country Park

The South Wales Portland Cement and Lime Company's works at Lower Penarth dug limestone from these quarries for manufacturing Portland Cement, Aberthaw Lime and, later on, for Ferrocrete. The works closed in 1969 and the 210 acre old limestone quarry remained derelict for several years. The 1971 Countryside Act permitted local authorities to establish Country Parks so the Vale of Glamorgan and South Glamorgan agreed in 1975 to embark jointly on establishing such a Park in the coastal area between Penarth and Barry where both stressed the need to keep a green wedge of countryside. So in 1976 the quarries were compulsory purchased to create a country park. The Welsh Committee of the Countryside Commission for England and Wales visited the site to see if it was a scheme they could properly support. A joint application by the South Glamorgan County Council and the Vale of Glamorgan Borough Council was made to initiate work to facilitate its development. The idea was generally accepted although one local Councillor thought it would become a haven for drugs use.

The Country Park now has many attractions, including a grassy areas for games, barbecues, a boadwalk, a nature reserve and a children's play area. There is also the 13/14th century abandoned Medieval village at Cosmeston which was excavated over a number of years by the Glamorgan/Gwent Archaeological Trust. Now many of the buildings have been reconstructed on the basis of the excavated stone footings to give a good idea of a peasant farmers settlement sometime before the Black Death.

The Country Park with the Medieval village has become a popular place, although there is currently concern over possible chemical pollution through past dumping of waste within the site.

Railway Walk

When the line to the Cement Works was closed in 1969, the linear strip between Penarth Town and Lower Penarth was then available for other purposes. There is now the footpath leading to Cosmeston Country Park and the grassed open space between Sully Terrace and Arthur Terrace. Some of the station seats were purchased by the Council for public use with one conveniently situated half way up Beach Hill.

Stanwell Road Garden - A missed opportunity

In September 1926 the Council suggested that a patch of earth against the wall of the Washington Hotel on the corner of Stanwell and Hickman Roads should be paved. Councillor Hallet, however, suggested here was an opportunity to create a small garden to greet visitors as they came out of the station. Although the idea seemed a good one it did not generally find favour because most Councillors thought the area was too small for this purpose. The Surveyor was asked instead to look into the matter with a view to providing a seat. When the matter of a garden was revived in October the Council finally decided instead to pave the area thereby moving the Penarth Times to print:

A councillor dreamt of a garden
Oh such a wonderful dream;
Of course we beg his pardon
But that garden would be a scream.

He imagined the love-birds cooing
'Midst flowers in this charming abode
But can you imagine them wooing
At the bottom of Hickman Road.

This was really a rather an unkind comment considering that Hickman Road itself was often referred to enthusiastically by the Press as Penarth's 'Unter Den Linden' because then, as now, most of the trees were limes.

Plymouth Park - A future opportunity

There are plans for this new park to be laid out on the infilled part of Penath Dock (Camlin, Lonsdale, Landscape Architects). It has received planning permission, but neither Cardiff Bay Development Corporation not the Vale of Glamorgan Council has any money available for its early initiation. It would be a great shame if the plan came to nothing.

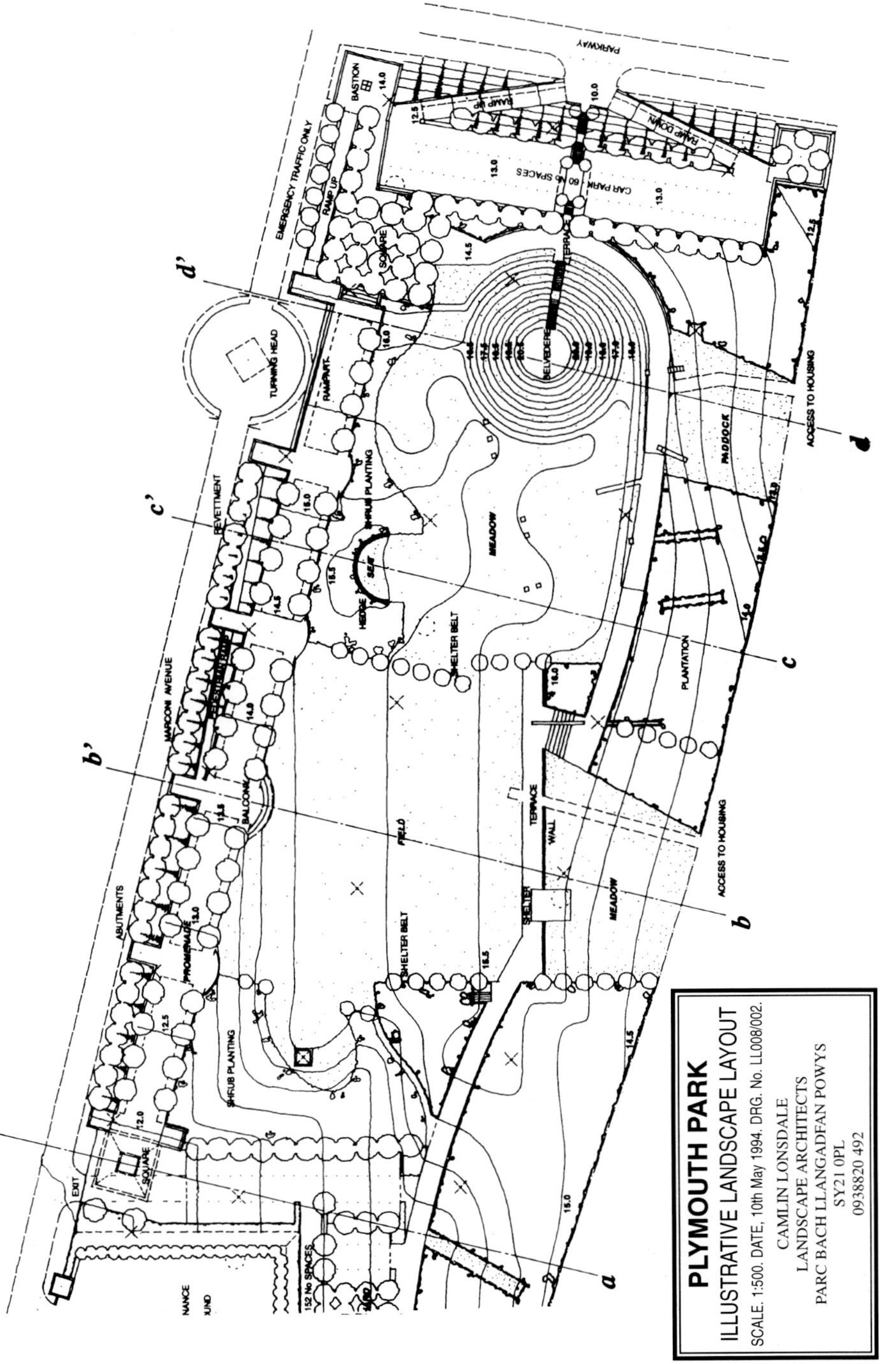
PARKWAY
BASTION
EMERGENCY TRAFFIC ONLY
RAMP UP
RAMP DOWN
CAR PARK - 60 No SPACES
SQUARE
TERRACE
BELVEDERE
TURNING HEAD
RAMPART
SHRUB PLANTING
MEADOW
PADDOCK
ACCESS TO HOUSING
REVETTMENT
SEAT
HEDGE
SHELTER BELT
PLANTATION
MARCONI AVENUE
BALCONY
FIELD
WALL
SHELTER
ABUTMENTS
PROMENADE
EXIT
152 No SPACES
PLYMOUTH PARK
ILLUSTRATIVE LANDSCAPE LAYOUT
SCALE. 1:500. DATE, 10th May 1994. DRG. No. LL008/002.
CAMLIN LONSDALE
LANDSCAPE ARCHITECTS
PARC BACH LLANGADFAN POWYS
SY21 0PL
0938820 492

THE FUTURE

Penarth's sea side vista was developed with an overall picture in mind. Over the last thirty or so years it has been severely altered and destroyed to many peoples minds. The loss of the Esplanade Hotel, the imposition of stark concrete flats and car park on the front and the alteration of the Bridgeman Road skyline have shown two things. People want a sea view and the planners have let them get their view to the detriment of Penarth's Victorian and Edwardian heritage.

Penarth is still a garden by sea. Windsor Gardens are now nearly 120 years old, we have celebrated the centenary of the pier. Soon Penarth Head Open Space and Alexandra Gardens will be 100 years old and the Italian Gardens will be 75 years old. But they have all had mixed histories of success and near failure. The bandstand and the shelter have gone from Alexandra Park and think what it would be like to still have the dingle bridge in Windsor Gardens. There was even talk of 'developing' the Italian Gardens into a block of flats when the other concrete buildings were going up along the front.

So what of the future? Financial decisions in the Vale Council are leaving parks open all the time unless a 'local arrangement' can be made, which means finding a volunteer. So far there have been no problems but will this attitude in the long term save what is left of our *Garden by the Sea*?

Like so many other people, I have played and walked in the parks and then taken my son there to do the same. I can only hope that future generations will be able to continue enjoying the pleasures that the town fathers thoughtfully provided for us.

BIBLIOGRAPHY

Benjamin E. A.: *Penarth 1841-71*. D. Brown & Sons Ltd., Cowbridge and Bridgend, Glamorgan. 1980.

Bevan E.T.: *Old Penarth*. 1949.

Carradice P. : *Penarth Pier 1894-1994*. Baron. 1994.

Carradice P. & Best G.: *Beside the Seaside: South Wales in Camera*. Quotes Ltd. 1992.

Coombes N.: *Passenger Steamers of the Bristol Channel. A pictorial Record*. Twelveheads Press. 1990.

Craig R The ports and shipping. *Glamorgan County History*. V. Chapter X pp.468-518. 1980.

Gibbs J.M.: *James Pyke Thompson. The Turner House, Penarth* National Museum of Wales. 1990.

Hilling J.B. The buildings of Llandaff, Penarth and outer Cardiff: an historical survey. Glamorgan Historian 7, 102-147. 1971.

Ings D.G.: *Penarth in old picture postcards*. European Library - Zaltbommel/Netherlands. 1985.

Ings D.G.: *Penarth in old picture postcards volume 2*. European Library - Zaltbommel/Netherlands. 1990.

Jenkins J.G. & Jenkins D. *Cardiff Shipowners*. National Museum of Wales. 1988.

Linnard W. 'Lord' Forrest of St Fagans: Estate Agent extraordinary. The Journal of Glamorgan History 33, 55-68. 1989.

Mountford E & Spinks N.: *The Taff Vale lines to Penarth*. Oakwood Press. 1993.

Newman J. *The buildings of Wales: Glamorgan*. Penguin Books & University of Wales Press. 1995

Thorne R.: *Penarth - A history*. The Starling Press Ltd. Risca, Gwent, Vol.1 1975; vol.2 1976.

Tilney C.: *A history of the Parish of Penarth with Lavernock (Revised edition)*. 1988.

Minutes of the Penarth Town Council and Penarth Urban District Council - Public Records Office, Cardiff.

The Penarth Times.

The Penarth News.

The Penarth Observer.

The Western Mail.

The South Wales Echo.